Making Miniature
Period Furniture
for Dolls' Houses

Angela Law

Making Miniature
Period Furniture
for Dolls' Houses

THE CROWOOD PRESS

CONTENTS

INTRODUCTION

This book is aimed at collectors of 1:12 scale miniatures and artisans with a basic understanding of miniatures and miniature making. It also provides tips and techniques for producing miniatures that look like antiques without the need to be an expert in crafts such as carpentry, carving, engraving or leather working, or buying expensive pieces of kit and materials. This book will also direct miniaturists old and new towards some of the more advanced skills and techniques.

There are twelve projects to explore in this book. Ten of the projects come with their own plan and instructions for the reader to follow; the other two are freer 'inspiration' projects that focus on repurposing a particular object, and come with instructions and suggestions that can be adapted as required.

More advanced miniature makers can simply incorporate some of their own techniques and skills when tackling the projects in this book. Hopefully, they too will find some interesting new ideas and tips to add to their current knowledge base.

GETTING YOUR MINIATURIST JOURNEY STARTED

Miniatures surround us all in our daily lives in some shape or form, for example in the toys you give your children or the holiday decorations that go on your Christmas tree. Many of us will have worn jewellery or owned keyrings that incorporate a miniature of something important to us. Five thousand years ago, the ancient Egyptians were making miniatures of loved ones, servants and possessions to take with them to the afterlife, while in war rooms throughout history, miniature battlefields have been used to plan and deploy manoeuvres against the enemy. They are often invaluable in film and TV – think of the opening credits of *Game of Thrones*, or the scenes from *Gladiator* with the beautiful little effigies of Maximus's wife and child.

Dolls' houses and dolls' house furniture also offer a way of escaping into another world (albeit a smaller one) that resembles our own but offers so many avenues to explore, including history and design. Miniatures can depict any period from Roman and Tudor to Victorian to the 1960s. This book will show you how to give free rein to your own artistic expression in creating a little world that is all your own. Where else can you have a castle within a manor house within a house, or an actual rocket in your pocket?

The twelve projects in this book (fitting, as you are exploring 1:12 scale) provide an introduction to the world of 1:12 scale miniatures. Be it handmade, scratch built and/or repurposed dolls' houses and miniatures that piqued your interest, I hope you will leave this book with new ideas with how to bring your creative concepts to fruition.

The projects are mainly wood based, because it is easily obtainable, versatile and forgiving – make

Rosary bead, 1525–1550. (Metropolitan Museum of Art, New York)

Terracotta doll with articulated arms dating from the fourth century BC. (Metropolitan Museum of Art, New York)

a mistake and you can easily rub it down or turn it into something else. Many of the methods shown in this book can however be used with other materials.

All these projects are intended for competent adults or young people with strict adult supervision only. All tools and materials should be used following the manufacturer's safety guidelines, and all the pieces you can make are collector's pieces (not toys) and are not suitable for children or pets.

MOVING FORWARD

You do not need to be a certified historian or a trained woodworker to make historical pieces. Part of the joy of making antique-style miniatures is learning their place in history and the techniques used along the way. Do not be afraid to think outside the box and add your own touches: after all, that is how any art thrives – there are no set rules, just some basic guidelines on how to get started.

It is not the aim of this book to show you how to do perfect carvings, lathing, pyrography (writing with fire) and so on; as Marilyn Monroe once said, 'imperfection is beauty'. Here you will be given the basic principles and some simple designs that you can make and develop into more complex pieces should you choose to do so, with more complex techniques, tools and skills that you may have already or will learn on your miniature journey – for example carving, or using the lathe for pillars and columns.

We will talk about which tools you need to get started and which tools you may wish to purchase as your skills progress, such as a lathe or pyrography machines. Always start with lower-priced options so that you can decide if you wish to develop your skills in a specific area first, and only invest in more expensive kit when you're happy that is the direction you want to go in.

This book starts by showing you some simple methods and materials that you can use to give your furniture/interior pieces that aged appearance that can give your work the look and feel of an antique piece. You will be given an insight into how to finish not only dolls' house furniture pieces but larger projects such as room boxes and dolls' houses just like the one shown here, which was made in 2008 but is often mistaken for a Georgian or Victorian piece – which is exactly the result I was aiming for. When someone asks you about the provenance of your piece, you know you are on the right track.

SOURCES OF INSPIRATION

If you were fortunate enough as a child to have visited places such as Windsor Castle and the Tower of London, you may still remember the sense of wonder they evoked – and that feeling does not fade for adults. These buildings have captured the essence of past inhabitants and seem in their energy to want to share the secrets held within their walls, often made more powerful by the wonderfully preserved interior decorations and furniture (showing craftsmanship of old) held within them.

For historical context, the focus of this book is mainly on the UK, which has a rich and diverse mix of wonderfully maintained historical sites and buildings. There are many houses, castles and sites throughout the country that will give you an enchanting fly-on-the-wall perspective of amazing

Historical-looking dolls' house made in 2008.

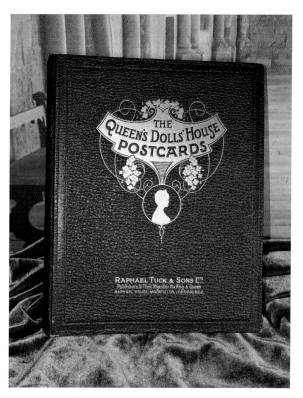

The Queen's Dolls' House Postcards, published by Raphael Tuck & Sons Ltd in 1924, contained postcards of 48 objects in the dolls' house. Author's own copy.

Some of the images from *The Queen's Dolls' House Postcards* book. Author's own copy.

interiors, furniture and way of life in times gone by. You can whip out your phone to take photographs or do a quick sketch at these sites as a reference point for pieces you may wish to make in the future. Attached gift shops will also often have picture postcards, books and novelties that make useful reference points for future projects.

One place that will be of huge inspiration for your future miniature furniture pieces is Hever Castle, family home of the Boleyn family. Each room in this beautiful castle is full of wonderful pieces of furniture and architecture that cannot help but get the creative juices flowing. The Waldegrave Room alone has multiple pieces of Tudor furniture, including a four-poster bed, blanket box, chairs and cabinet as well as a lovely fireplace and panel work. A huge bonus for miniature-lovers and artisans alike is that the castle also houses a collection of 1:12 scale miniature model houses from the late

master English miniaturist furniture maker John J. Hodgson.

Bowood House is an absolute must-visit for eighteenth-century furniture inspiration, with its beautiful interiors by Robert Adam, the British neoclassical architect and interior designer. It is a grand house with beautiful gardens, but manages to be welcoming rather than overwhelming. The libraries and many beautiful bookcases in this house have given many a miniature maker a starting point for their projects.

At St Fagans National Museum of History in Cardiff, there are more than 40 original buildings re-erected in the grounds from different historical periods, including a farm, a school and a sixteenth-century manor house complete with beautiful furniture and interiors.

Not in the UK, but well worth visiting if you have the opportunity, the Rijksmuseum in Amsterdam

Hever Castle, the double-moated thirteenth-century home of Anne Boleyn. (Hever Castle & Gardens)

The Waldegrave Room in Hever Castle. (Hever Castle & Gardens)

Not only is Hever Castle a historical delight in itself, but it is also home to the amazingly detailed collection of 1:12 scale miniature model houses by the late master English miniature furniture maker, John J. Hodgson. (Hever Castle & Gardens)

Bowood House in Wiltshire. (Anna Stowe)

holds some magnificent pieces of art as well as miniatures and historical pieces of furniture, including the Petronella Oortman dolls' house, famous for its exact proportions and use of authentic materials.

In fact, being able to visit historical sites online (often even with a 360-degree tour) is one of the benefits of the internet for the model maker; for example, you can see Windsor Castle or take a look at the fourteenth-century tithe barn in Pilton (no furniture here but stunning beamed ceiling work), or indeed the Rijksmuseum in Amsterdam, without leaving the comfort of your own home. The National Trust is just one of the sites that offers you a huge database of historical buildings across the UK that you can explore online. Wikipedia is also great for a more detailed description of historical sites, and sometimes has direct web links to related sites.

Social media sites such as Instagram and Pinterest are good for viewing other people's work and sharing ideas and images; these are good places to find like-minded individuals with whom to explore more specific areas of interest, whether it be an interest in Tudor history or 1920s furniture. If you have hit a snag in your work, you can ask fellow enthusiasts

Robert Adam died in March 1792 and is buried in the South Transept of Westminster Abbey – a testament to his talent and achievement. At his death he left almost 9,000 drawings, which were purchased in 1833 for £200 by the architect John Soane and can now be found at the wonderful Sir John Soane's Museum in London (another great place to visit).

Robert Adam, 1728–1792. (National Portrait Gallery, London)

how they dealt with the particular issue. YouTube videos are also a wonderful resource for learning how to work with certain tools and materials.

BRIEF HISTORY OF FURNITURE STYLES

This timeline provides an overview of the different historical periods that can be recreated by most 1:12 scale miniature makers, focusing specifically on the evolution of the bed, as the core piece of domestic furniture: as Napoleon Bonaparte said, 'The bed has become a place of luxury to me! I would not exchange it for all the thrones in the world.'

Medieval Period

Broadly speaking, this period covers the time from the fall of the Roman empire up to the Tudor accession in the fifteenth century, but little survives from the earlier part of this era, partly because relatively little furniture was made at this time and partly because wood is perishable. What surviving pieces we do have are generally from the thirteenth century or later. From the fifteenth century, panelling on chests and cupboards became common, often decorated with linenfold and brightly painted or gilded.

Box beds were perfect for keeping in the heat during the cold winters and keeping out rodents and insects all year round. Examples of fifteenth-century box beds have been found all over the place – for example, Russia and the Netherlands, as well as in Cornwall, Devon and Wales in the UK. This type of furniture was popular worldwide for both the rich and the poor due to its simple construction – basically a box with a front opening. The wealth of the owner would have determined the type of wood used and the level of carving or decoration the frame would have had, as well as the quality of the mattress and cushions, and inner drapes (if there were any, for extra warmth and privacy). This type of bed would often be accompanied with a matching (in decoration), often panelled, blanket box and perhaps even a cradle. These items were passed on and used well into the seventeenth and eighteenth centuries.

The Petronella Oortman cabinet dolls' house dates from the seventeenth century. (Rijksmuseum, Amsterdam)

Four-poster beds were also popular during this period and would often be highly carved and, again, for the wealthier classes would have matching furniture such as high-back chairs (some with arched backs) and a huge blanket box, often placed at the end of the bed and used to store extra bedding.

The half tester bed was similar in construction to the four-poster bed but without the posts at the foot end and a simple canopy extending about a third of the length of the bed from the head posts. Both four-poster and half tester beds were often used to show off wealth to visitors. The owners would decorate their beds in lavish drapes of heavy silk and velvet with beautiful rope ties along with equally heavy and intricately detailed bedding. Often a guest would be led straight to the bed, and conversations, meals and business meetings would be held from it.

Showing the place that you slept in to your guests was an indication of high social standing.

Tudor Period

The first ruler of the Tudor dynasty was Henry VII (1485–1509) and the last was Elizabeth I (1558–1603).

Tudor furniture, including bedposts, chair legs and table legs, was heavily carved (mainly from oak), often with flamboyant designs and scenes. There was often also painted decoration very much in the spirit of the English Renaissance (often referred to as Elizabethan). Almost every surface would be carved, turned and/or inlaid. The wealthier citizens would have homes filled with wall panelling (again sometimes heavily carved), ceiling panels and decorations, all carved from wood.

Some of Britain's most beautiful woodwork and carpentry is from the Tudor period and survives in many of the great houses and castles. Compared to today's modern furniture, these pieces are very heavy and, in most cases, take up a lot of room. Sideboards were often used to display plates and silverware in a show of wealth. At this time the feather mattress first made an appearance, replacing the harsher straw one, and would have fitted in the four-poster bed that was a must-have for those who could afford it.

Truckle and trundle beds first became popular in the sixteenth century. The main bed would have usually been a double of some sort – if you were lucky, a four-poster. Underneath the main bed was enough space for a sliding (wheeled) platform that you could pull out when you needed it (basically a bed underneath a bed), for example for a guest.

Members of poorer households would rest upon the roped or woven strapped area of their truckle bed without a mattress but hopefully with a sheet and blanket. The extremely poor would make do with simple blocks of hay laid on the floor or on a raised platform (to avoid vermin).

Many pieces of furniture of this time were expensive and would therefore often be considered as heritage pieces that would be passed down through the family for generations.

One especially magnificent bed from this period is the Great Bed of Ware, which is housed in the Victoria and Albert Museum in London. Over 3m wide, it is said to comfortably sleep up to seven or eight people. It was made in 1590, probably as a tourist attraction piece for an inn in Ware, Hertfordshire, and soon became famous – it was even referenced by William Shakespeare in *Twelfth Night*.

Stuart Period

Jacobean style (1600–1690) followed the English Early Renaissance, and takes its name from Elizabeth's successor, James I. Furniture from this time is often extremely heavy, characterised by straight lines, ornate carvings, and a dark finish – in fact, not at all dissimilar to Tudor style. Box beds, for example were still very much in use (the Rijksmuseum in Amsterdam has a fine oak example dating from the first half of the seventeenth century). These pieces were built to last. Skills in carving and tool making had developed, however,

The Great Bed of Ware made in 1590, shown here without bedding and curtains. Look carefully, and you may even spot the ancient graffiti carved into the bedposts (not notches) by just some of its lucky occupants. (Victoria and Albert Museum, London)

so we find more intricate posts and chair legs
as a result.

The Restoration

During the reign of William and Mary (1689–1702),
lighter, taller and more delicate styles started to
appear, and furniture acquired distinct Dutch and
Chinese influence. Pieces often stood upon trumpet-
turned legs supported by Spanish-style ball feet, and
were decorated in beautiful oriental lacquerwork,
often finished with heavy teardrop drawer pulls.
Furniture often had a lighter framework with more
elaborate hangings and upholstery, such as valances,
drapes, chair backings and elaborate bedding, like
the Dutch Rosendael bed shown here. Some beds
would be topped with plumes of feathers bursting
from the top of each of the bedposts and could
be painted with beautiful scenes of landscapes
and gardens.

Queen Anne ruled from 1702 to 1714, but what we
think of as Queen Anne furniture started to emerge
during William and Mary's time. Typical features
were cabriole legs upon pad or drake feet, fiddle-
backed chairs (so named because they resemble
the outline of a violin) and bat-wing-shaped drawer
pulls, which are still popular today.

Georgian Period

Louis XVI (1760–1789) style was designed for
Marie Antionette and was heavily influenced by

The Rosendael bed, a seventeenth-century four-poster bed
made of pine wood, wallpapered with plain and chiselled velvet.
(Rijksmuseum, Amsterdam)

Author's own sketch of a William and Mary side table.

neoclassical themes, evident in the straight lines,
columns with classical motifs (such as urns and
fluting and classical depictions) and highly carved
detailing.

Preparatory
drawing for a
Chippendale
sofa, 1759.
(Metropolitan
Museum of
Art, New York)

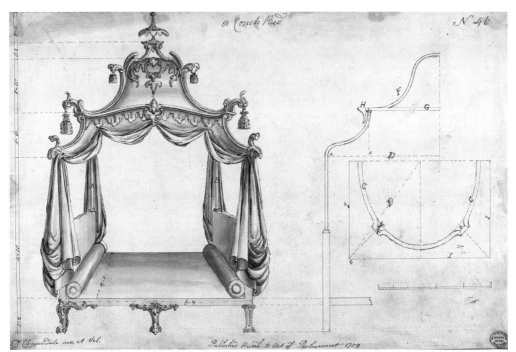

Preparatory
drawing for a
Chippendale
couch
bed, 1759.
(Metropolitan
Museum of
Art, New York)

Thomas Chippendale (1718–1779) was a cabinetmaker from London. The furniture style that bears his name encompasses a range of influences such as Gothic, Chinese, Queen Anne and French, and is notable for its cabriole legs, and ball and claw feet. Chippendale tall cabinets (often referred to as highboys) and cases often have a broken pediment or bonnet top.

Like Chippendale, Hepplewhite furniture is named after its creator. George Hepplewhite (1727–1786) was also a cabinetmaker based in London; his designs were characterised by neoclassical influences and were elegant and delicate in form. Hepplewhite chairs had tapered legs and beautiful contrasting inlaid veneers, and often a shield-shaped back. The style was much admired in the USA.

Although still rather opulent in the wealthier households, eighteenth-century beds were often less heavy-looking than those of previous centuries, with more delicate finials and decorations. Still on a grand scale were the four-poster beds of the very wealthy with more fabrics and additions (feathers and swags) than ever. This emphasis on fabric also applied to chairs, which would be upholstered not only on the seat area but also on the backs. Headboards and footboards of beds were more likely to be decorated with padded, tapestried or striped fabrics (something we still see in more modern pieces today) rather than heavy carving.

Metal beds were becoming more popular as well. Meanwhile, hay-filled mattresses were being replaced with cotton-filled ones, but still supported either by a solid base or a system of wool straps and/or ropes.

To see some eighteenth-century furniture in situ, visit Bowood House, a Grade I-listed Georgian country house in Wiltshire with interiors by Robert Adam (see opposite). There are fine examples of Georgian ceilings, furniture and bookcases, as well as stunning fireplaces to be seen.

MASS PRODUCTION

The Industrial Revolution, which spanned roughly the mid-eighteenth to the mid-nineteenth century, brought many changes to manufacturing. New machinery meant furniture could be produced on larger scales and faster and more cheaply than ever before. This was good news for the servants during this time, as they were more likely to have access to a simple metal or wooden bed to sleep on rather than having to sleep on the floor or on a pallet.

GOTHIC REVIVAL

Gothic revival style furniture was popular in both the eighteenth and nineteenth centuries. It drew its inspiration from the Middle Ages and was characterised by features such as pointed arches, lacy carvings and fretwork.

Sheraton style is named after English designer George Sheraton (1751–1806), along with Chippendale and Hepplewhite one of the three greats of Georgian furniture design. His work is similar to that of Hepplewhite in its methods and materials. Both artisans used contrasting veneers, and often had elegant, tapered legs supporting their pieces. Sheraton's work is distinguished by its simplicity and straight lines.

Hepplewhite style was very popular in the early USA, where it essentially merged with Sheraton to create the Federal style (popular between 1780 and 1820). Federal furniture also has simple straight lines with contrasting veneers, sometimes with neoclassical motifs.

Pennsylvania Dutch (1720–1830) is another typical American furniture style, this time with Germanic influences introduced by immigrant German furniture makers. This variant is characterised by its total simplicity in style and the beautiful folk paintings often used for decoration.

Library at Bowood House. (Diane Vose Photography)

Characterised by classical ornamentation and simple carvings, the French-inspired style of furniture known as American Empire (1800–1840) was popular in the USA. Pieces often had simple columns carved on each side of the drawers.

Victorian Period

During Queen Victoria's reign (1837–1901), furniture started to be produced on a large scale, thanks to the progress made in manufacturing during the Industrial Revolution. Victorian furniture is usually heavy in its proportions with a dark finish (sometimes black), and often had romantic influences and ornamentation, such as carved flowers.

While a lot of beds were still passed down as heritage pieces in large period houses and in wealthier families, designers were coming up with beautiful styles and pieces of furniture that even the working class could aim to purchase (mainly because pieces no longer had to be individually designed and built, thus reducing the cost). The bed would still have been expensive but not necessarily out of one's reach.

Fortunately, trees such as pine and birch were bountiful during this period, which meant that a good carpenter or someone who was good with their hands could build a simple, sturdy

Author's own quick sketch of a nineteenth-century French cherry-wood bed.

bed following simple instructions (a little like a nineteenth-century Ikea).

The simple sketch here depicts a nineteenth-century French bed made from cherry wood. Similar examples from the same period can be found made from pine and birch. People were able to create their own affordable versions of the beds slept in by the wealthy as the tools and materials more readily available to them. This style of bed is still popular today.

Highly influenced by the ideas and methods of British artist and author William Morris, the Arts and Crafts movement (1880–1910) focused on good

design partnered with excellent craftmanship. Morris and his followers developed furniture that moved away from the heavy traditional Victorian style, creating uncluttered pieces that had clean and simple lines and combined with strong form and function.

Twentieth Century
Art Deco (1910–1939) originated from France just before World War I and is characterised by bold, vibrant colours and distinctive geometric shapes and patterns.

FANTASY

Fantasy pieces are timeless. The Greeks and Romans had their mythical beasts, the Egyptians had their sphynx and the Georgians their classical gods. Why not let your imagination run wild? Perhaps you have a slight penchant for cherubs and the putti (which could fit medieval or Tudor settings onwards) or you have a fondness for dragons or griffins – whatever your fantastical preference, you can incorporate it into your designs.

MOURNING FURNITURE

Queen Victoria went into a long period of mourning after the loss of her beloved Albert and was known for wearing her famed black mourning dresses. This mourning was also expressed in interiors, and it was common for households to have black furniture pieces and black fireplaces (often with a metal surround that was also black). Of course, there was also a practical element to this, as it would disguise any soot marks from burning wood and coal.

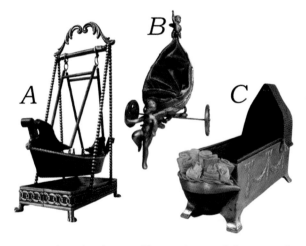

Pieces with varying degrees of fantasy elements. A: Regency-style swing boat with fantasy elements; B: The Fairy King's Throne, a full fantasy piece; C: Cot in Tudor style with fantasy elements.

A QUICK GUIDE TO 1:12 SCALE

This is the scale most commonly used today by makers of dolls' houses and miniature furniture, and is therefore the scale used for the projects in this book. Some miniaturists do however use other scales, such as 1:6, 1:16, 1:24 and 1:48.

One of the most famous dolls' houses in 1:12 scale, with furniture examples still on display today, at Windsor Castle, is Queen Mary's Dolls' House, designed by architect Sir Edwin Lutyens and built in the early 1920s (*see* pictures earlier in the chapter). The dolls' house contains pieces designed specifically for the house by known designers, including Cartier (a longcase clock), Fabergé (a mouse), Chubb (safe), Royal School of Needlework (tester bed) and Weaving School for Crippled Girls, Stratford-upon-Avon (a carpet).

A must-see (in person or online) for all miniaturists is the dolls' house, mentioned earlier, of Petronella Oortman (built between 1686 and 1710), at the Rijksmuseum in Amsterdam. This dolls' house was the inspiration for the wonderful 2014 novel *The Miniaturist* by English author Jessie Burton, which was later adapted into a BBC miniseries. Watch the TV show to see some beautiful 1:12 scale miniatures.

Both the above dolls' houses give a good visual guide for what 1:12 scale looks like, including architecture, fixtures and fittings, furniture and accessories.

One-twelfth scale means the model is one-twelfth of the size of the real-life object. This particular ratio was developed as a simple and effective way to size down our everyday objects because in British imperial measurements there are twelve inches in a foot (which is why you may also see it referred to as one-inch scale), so one foot in the real world becomes one inch in the model. The scale can be easily adapted to other scales such as 1:6 and 1:24 by using two inches or half an inch per foot respectively.

So, for example, most 1:12 scale dolls houses will have doors that are approximately 7½in high, which compare to full-size doors that are 7½ft high. This rule is not set in stone for either fixtures and fittings or furniture, however, and the scale police will not come for you if you are not exact. We all know that furniture sizes do vary – even nowadays we have king-size and queen-size beds – but scale should always be considered, especially in relation to the space the piece will occupy and when finishing its decoration.

The Rijksmuseum in Amsterdam. (IMAGE COURTESY OF THE UNITED STATES LIBRARY OF CONGRESS PRINTS AND PHOTOGRAPHS)

Furniture Sizing Guide for 1:12 Scale: *Measurements in inches*

BEDROOM

	Height	Width	Depth
Twin Bed	2.75	3.25	6.5
Double Bed	2.75	4.5	6.5
Day Bed	2.75	3	6.5
King Bed	2.75	6	6.75
Queen Bed	2.75	5	6.75
Four Poster Bed	5.9/6	4.9-6	6.5-7
Cradle	3.25	4.35	2.35
Bedside Stand	2.5	2	2
Dressing Table	2.5	5	1.75
Tallboy	5	3	2
Vanity Table	2.25	3.5	1.5

LIVING ROOM

	Height	Width	Depth
Sofa	3	7	3
Knoll Sofa	4/4.5	7	3
Loveseat	3	5	3
Armchair	3	2.75	2.75
Sofa Table	2.5	2	2
Tall Bookcase	6	3	1
Piano	3.5	5	Varies

OFFICE

Tall Bookcase	6	3	1
Desk	2.5	4	2.5
Bench	3	4	3
Desk Chair	3.5	1.5	1.5

DINING ROOM

	Height	Width	Depth
Six Seater Table	2.5	6	3
Four Seater Table	2.5	4	3
Round Table	2.5	3	3
Dining Chairs	3	1.5	1.5
Buffet	3	6	2
Dresser	6	6	2

BATHROOM

	Height	Width	Depth
Bathtub	2	2.5/3	5
Toilet	Varies	Varies	Varies

Note: These measurements are simply as a guide. Some items vary significantly due to style/design. Also depending on the setting you can go bigger on some items, as you would in your own home eg. if you have tall ceilings and can therefore build higher and perhaps wider bookcases or if you desire a a longer dining table to seat more people in a larger room setting.

A basic furniture sizing guide for 1:12 scale.

There are many free printable sheets of 1:12 and other scale miniatures that you can easily find with an online search; these will provide you with a good reference guide to be going on with and you can adapt to your setting accordingly.

A simple 1:12 scale furniture guideline is shown here. These sizes are a guide only, and you may wish to go bigger for larger houses or castles. Always keep your legs, posts and finials to the correct scale, though, as it will look odd if your chair legs are too chunky or the pattern on your woodwork is too big. A bedpost twice the size of your 1:12 scale doll's head is most likely to look a little strange unless you are going for a modern or sci-fi look.

Scales such as 1:12 can be measured in any type of measurements, including cm or mm. There are many online measurement calculators that can help with this.

Each of the plans for the projects in this book are to be used as guides and not as templates, but always follow the measurements. It is advisable with handmade pieces to always do a dry run of putting your pieces together (using paper tape or 3M-type medical tape); this will enable you to make any adjustments before using wood glues and/or permanent adhesives.

CHAPTER 1

TOOLS, EQUIPMENT AND MATERIALS

n this chapter you will find advice on a range of tools that are easy to source and are widely available for miniature making projects and applications. You will be given a brief outline/description for each tool and some of its applications. The types of tool covered will be ones that require a higher level of human interaction than the tool itself – so no 3D printers or laser cutters. You may wish to explore these options later, as they are perfect for miniaturists who prefer the analytical design element of the craft in its precise form rather than the hands-on approach. This book focuses on tools that will help you with the latter.

ESSENTIAL ITEMS

Tools

- Craft knife, craft swivel knife, Stanley or Rolson knife, plus spare blades
- Small hacksaw, bow saw or coping saw – there are many available, but make sure you use the correct blades for the material you are cutting
- Tin shears or metal cutter – projects in this book use FatMax tin shears
- Sharp crafting scissors (for card)
- Small hand-drill – either a small electric one (such as the Dremel 3000 multi-tool or the older model 7700), or a manual one (such as The Army Painter miniature and model drill)
- Small drill bits (about 0.1mm–1.2mm in size) for creating tiny wormholes and smaller holes for

dowels; search for terms such as 'micro twist drill bits' or 'craft/model-making drill bits'
- Drill gauge for measuring hole sizes for dowel rod applications
- Sanding blocks or sponges and/or hand sander for wet and dry sanding in coarse, medium and fine for use on metal and wood
- Sanding files – semicircular file and squared file
- Mini wood planer – this may be useful if you have any uneven edges on thinner woods that have been cut by hand
- Needle files – curved or squared and flat
- Metal ruler with finger guard
- Small hammer and nails
- Small paintbrushes
- Meat tenderiser

Equipment

- Cutting mat or board, placed on a solid surface, ideally some sort of workbench
- Solid worktop or workbench
- Workbench chair to protect your spine. I stand for about 50 per cent of my work so it is good to have a decent chair for designing and finishing pieces to reduce bending over intricate work. Try to get one with a good rating (see what other crafters say) that gives good spine support. A hydraulic chair is easily height adjustable
- LED/daylight work lamp with magnifier
- Safety clothing – cut-proof gloves and apron, and hair ties for longer hair

- Safety mask and goggles – always wear an appropriate safety mask when cutting or sawing woods and using adhesives, wood stains, paints and sealants
- Fire extinguisher that is appropriate for the setting and purpose – always follow the manufacturer's safety guidance and instructions
- Inkjet printer (ideally with a scanner)
- Camera
- Weights or tins for holding pieces in place while glue dries

Materials
- 2mm-thick wood sheets/craft panels, often called balsa or plywood; the choice of wood is yours – lime wood and pine are both widely available and are easy to cut, colour and stain
- 4mm-thick wood sheets/craft panels
- Bamboo skewer sticks for edging
- Rattan (diffuser) sticks, which are also great for edging and come in many colours; they are easy to cut with scissors
- Bamboo sticks or strips (available from most crafting stores), approximately 30cm–40cm long, 9mm wide and 3mm thick
- Two oak wood rods, approximately 20cm long with a diameter of 15mm
- Two pine wood square sticks, approximately 30cm long × 10mm
- A4 sheets of solid cardboard (not corrugated), approximately 2mm thick
- Craft card for book inners – 380g/m² weight
- Thin card (like the type often inside shirt packaging)
- Printable canvas – for example, Simplicity PhotoFabric Cotton Poplin; alternatively, just use paper
- Printable parchment paper
- Cinnamon powder, for aging scrolls; alternatives would be tea or pepper

- Selection of finials – for example wood trims from previous projects, tooled leather, beads, fabric, red string (for books) and so on; 2mm and 4mm wooden craft beads are very handy and widely available
- Jewellery box corner feet, small hinges, and small door latch (usually in brass, bronze or silver) – *see* Chapter 14
- Repurposing pieces – for example a silver metal snuff tin, silver-metal gravy boat, tooled leather cigar box, old picture frames, silver-metal cigarette tin and old clock case
- Wood veneer sheets in 2mm and 4mm thickness
- Strong wood glue – for example Pattex Crocodile Power wood glue
- Industrial-grade superglue – for example either Everbuild HV transparent gel (for use on MDF, rubber, metal, PVC and plastic), which is better for MDF/wood, or the less viscous Everbuild GP CYN50 transparent (for MDF, rubber, metal, EPDM). Rite-Lok (MC100), by 3M, is also very good for metal joins
- Wood stain or scratch cover – for example Tableau Scratch Cover, which comes in various shades
- Wood scratch repair pens
- Gold and silver acrylic markers – for example Liquitex Professional acrylic marker pens in Iridescent Antique Gold
- Two-in-one sealant and varnish – a good one is Contura Aqua Solid 2in1
- Decorlack acrylic craft paint in Glossy Black
- Small tin of ivory paint for book inner edges
- Enamel paint – for example Revell 32180, Mud Brown Gloss
- Colour primer for metal – for example The Army Painter Colour Primer. You will need this as a key for the enamel topcoat, which will not grip well to the metal without it. Choose a colour closest to your chosen enamel topcoat

- Scrap tissue paper
- Alcohol wipes
- Fabric offcuts – for example old ties
- Tooled leather pieces – for example old cigarette/cigar boxes, thin belts, old bags/purses/wallets, old picture frames and trinket/jewellery boxes
- Pressed tin – for example trinket boxes or cigarette cases
- Mod Podge Antique Matte water-based sealer, glue, and finish
- Sticky tapes – strong double-sided sticky tape for fabric and card, paper tape (for example Tesa Eco, which is easy-tear and writable) and 3M medical tape (also easy to tear and remove and writable)
- Cotton buds
- Lint-free cloth or scrap cotton cloth for wiping away glue, wood stain, varnish residue and so on
- Miniature tiles or miniature tile sheet (optional)

This list may seem extensive, but it covers **all** projects in this book. Each individual project lists the actual tools and materials required to complete it. Bear in mind that you will often have plenty of material left over to use elsewhere, and of course tools can be used again and again.

NICE-TO-HAVE TOOLS

Most of the tools listed here are available from craft stores or online.

- Table saw
- Jigsaw
- Soldering iron – the one shown here by Weller is a mid-range kit, but you can find good kits on Amazon starting from around £20.
- Electric mitre saw or a small mitre block with saw – a huge time-saver
- Hand-carving tool kit

- Crafting tweezers – useful for removing tape and labels as well as wood shavings from constructed pieces, especially in hard-to-access areas
- Leather skiving knife for thinning any tooled leather being repurposed
- Tile cutter/s

TOOLS TO INVEST IN

This section focuses on tools that you can look at acquiring in the future to focus on specific areas of miniature making, such as using the lathe and pyrography. These will often help save time as well.

Do your research before you buy. You will find YouTube useful for ratings and ease of use as well as practical learning guides and tips.

Always start at the lower end of the price range for kit. The crafting lathe shown here, for example, will work perfectly well for 1:12 scale craft pieces like chair legs and bedposts. A pyrography machine from the cheaper end of the range at Amazon could be used later as a back-up machine if you do go on to invest in a more expensive model (always check customer reviews and ratings on purchases); it is only worth upgrading once you are sure that a particular technique is something you enjoy and wish to become more proficient in.

- Pyrography machine – the one shown here is one of my earlier kits, the Razertip SSD10; you can find kits from Amazon from £20
- Lathe for wood – shown here is the Proxxon Micro Lathe model DB 250
- Lathe for metal
- Table scroll saw – the model shown here is a Scheppach Deco-Flex which is perfect for crafting and is in the mid-price range at about £150–200. Project 12 introduces the option of using this type of scroll saw for cutting thicker pieces of wood

Workbench with clamp.

Table saw.

Soldering iron kit.

Mini electric mitre saw.

Hand carving tools.

Table scroll saw.

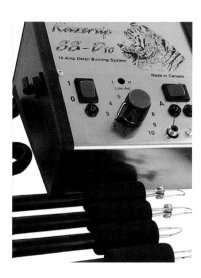

Pyrography machine.

Small lathe for wood.

- Leather tooling kit
- Leather punch/stamping machine – this will often serve multiple purposes such as embossing and holing as well; start with a DIY type, which looks a bit like a large lemon juicer and is often available on sites such as Amazon starting at around £100
- Engraving tools/router

ACQUIRING TOOLS

Always follow the manufacturers' recommendations on safety and usage. Research your intended purchase online and always check verified purchaser reviews. Make sure you purchase through a website and

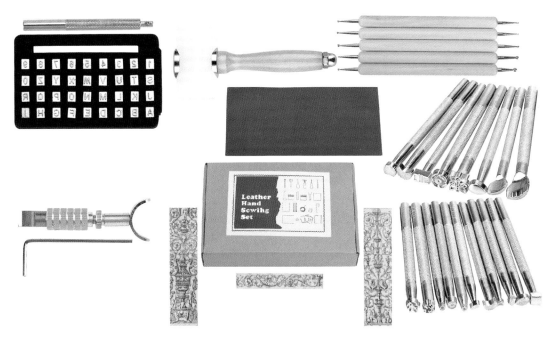

Leather-tooling kit.

payment method that offers payment protection and guarantees.

Some of the strongest and best-made hand tools are often over a hundred years old and can still be found at boot sales and second-hand markets. If in doubt of their condition, always ask someone with a knowledge of such items for their advice; when purchasing second-hand electrical tools, have these checked out by a qualified electrician before use.

SOURCING WOOD

Try to use scrap wood as much as possible. One of the best ways to do this is to use your own offcuts from projects (even the smallest offcuts can be turned into miniature firewood for fireplaces). Other sources for scrap wood are given below.

Online Simply search for 'scrap wood' on sites such as Etsy and eBay and you will find many a seller offering varying types and quantities. To find somewhere local, search for 'find scrap wood near me' or 'find free scrap wood near me' – you may be surprised at the number of places that offer it (such as the Bristol Wood Recycling project, for example).

Markets, car boot sales and second-hand shops
Look in baskets or through piles of broken cheaper items that the seller simply wants to get rid of, including items like wooden trinkets, jewellery, glove boxes and old clock cases (with or without clock). Car boot sales and markets are also a good source for old pieces of furniture that are beyond repair. Some charity shops in the UK, such as the British Red Cross and the YMCA, have their own furniture stores and here you will often find beautiful old wooden pieces that can be repurposed for 1:12 scale dolls' house and furniture projects. Always check, however, that you are not breaking up a piece that could be of value if restored.

Clock makers, cabinetmakers and furniture makers Do a little research to see if you have any local clock makers or cabinetmakers, or craft and art studios that could possibly have any scraps or offcuts that they may wish to dispose of. Offer to take any pieces they wish to be rid of – it may even help them with their environmental targets.

Universities and art schools It is worth investing a small amount of time to create an email template letter and send it out to your local universities and art schools offering to take some of their craft wood waste. Many universities and art schools that have woodworking shops will probably have their own solutions in place to dispose of waste, but these processes often have their own negative environmental effect (the energy it takes to incinerate and break down this type of waste is a drain on the planet's resources in itself). You may find some institutions will (regulations allowing) consider parting with some of their offcuts and rejected pieces in order to not only fulfil their own green agenda but also to help local artisans.

Reclamation yards These often have some great inspiration pieces; in any case, it is always worth asking, as they salvage pretty much everything. Again, check for local businesses online and email or phone first.

Post-consumer reclaimed This is waste wood from factory, commercial buildings and houses that has been saved from landfill. Search online.

Pre-consumer reclaimed This is waste from industrial processes such as manufacture of wood flooring and veneers and furniture making that never reached the consumer. It is worth doing a little research to find contact details for local businesses to see what they do with their offcuts, as you could

rescue useful pieces from being sent to landfill or the incinerator.

Orchard Salvage If you have a local orchard or forestry commission site, it is worth sending a standard email and or letter to see if they have any trees such as acacia or walnut that are no longer productive and need to be replaced. Ask them what they do with their removed trees. You will need to make sure they are not being disposed of due to disease before asking for anything, and make it clear you only want offcuts (not whole trees).

Forest floor salvage I often collect smaller wood pieces (branches and twigs) to cut into 1cm pieces for simple 1:12 scale firewood. I have found some beautiful tree branches that have been perfect for whittling and also for the lathe. Only gather naturally fallen pieces and make sure you are not on private land.

Driftwood Some beautiful pieces can be found on beaches or on riverbanks. These are often ideal as natural additions to a scene but can also be used for carvings. Again, you should be aware of any local regulations in relation to collecting driftwood or shells, especially if you are on private land. Also make sure you are not disturbing any local wildlife or insects by picking up any pieces – for example beavers and otters often dam up areas with pieces of wood to make sure their homes do not wash away.

Check your own house You will be surprised at the number of items you have in your own home that could be repurposed into miniatures. I recently found a damaged old Tallent 1950s trinket box that is perfect for refashioning into 1:12 scale wall panels or bed headboards. These boxes were mass produced in the 1950s and 1960s so are quite easy to find on auction sites.

An old damaged Tallent trinket box.

Purchasing New Wood Pieces

If you find that you have no other option but to buy new pieces of wood for a project (as will at times be the case), simply makes sure of the following:

Look for the FSC mark A sure-fire way of recognising sustainable wood is the FSC (Forest Stewardship Council) mark, as they are a non-profit and internationally recognised organisation. Woods that bear this mark come from companies that have had to prove responsible management of their timber-collection methods before gaining certification.

Online purchases If buying online, always check the listing to see if it confirms the wood is sourced environmentally and sustainably.

Sustainable forests Always aim to buy wood that is from sustainable forests such as pine, which is a tree that grows back fast and therefore helps to reduce the damage done by deforestation. Oak is also considered sustainable but does grow back more slowly than pine.

Do your research There are some woods you should avoid purchasing as they are in decline due to deforestation and, because they are slow-growing, are hard to sustain. One such wood is ebony, which takes at least a hundred years to mature. A good online search term is 'guide to buying sustainable wood'.

Bamboo Bamboo is one of the most sustainable woods as it has many species, grows very fast and can be cultivated without the use of chemicals. Even so, you should still try to source it via the International Network for Bamboo, as they will advise on what to look out for (purchase wise), as there has been large-scale destruction of bamboo habitats of giant pandas and mountain gorillas. Always check that the bamboo you are purchasing states that it is a sustainably sourced bamboo and that it is environmentally friendly. It is worth investing a little time to do your research, as, once you have found a reliable supplier, you are likely to purchase from them for many years to come. I use bamboo for much of my ceiling work and sometimes for basic edging of wall panels.

ENDANGERED WOODS

In this book there are some images of a dolls' house I made mainly from scrap rosewood that was over a hundred years old. Rosewood is now protected world-wide as it has been harvested almost to depletion. Always aim to use wood that has not been over-exploited, unless it is scrap wood for repurposing (such as damaged furniture). The list of endangered woods is constantly changing.

BRANDED TOOLS VERSUS NON-BRANDED

For some of the tools in the lists above, brand names have been included to give you a good basis for your own search for comparable tools. Always check a tool's specified applications and, where possible, its product rating and verified reviews before committing to purchase. Most of the tools suggested here are in the low- to mid-price range, and this is where the verified reviews come very much into play: if an item has plenty of positive reviews (even if it is not a recognised brand name), you can feel more confident about buying it. This is especially important if you are new to miniature making or are on a tight budget.

Wherever you buy your tools, make sure that you can return it for a refund or replacement if its performance does not deliver as expected.

It is still possible to find old and antique tools, which were often made to last by skilled craftsmen, and in many cases will still remain beyond our lifetimes. Look out for second-hand hammers, planes and whittling tools at markets and car boot sales. The only downside with purchasing old or antique tools is that they will generally not come with a guarantee, so you will need to rely on your own judgement and knowledge; if in doubt ask an expert.

SAFETY

Keep the following safety points in mind whenever working on your miniatures.

- The projects in this book are not suitable for children.
- When making miniatures, the lighting is even more important than for full-size pieces, so to avoid eye issues (dry eyes, styes, eye strain), make sure your workspace is well lit. Use a magnified light source for areas that require extra concentrated focus and always try to use lamps that provide as natural a light as possible. Take regular breaks if you are doing a lot of close detail work.
- All electrical equipment and outlets should be regularly checked and serviced. Make sure that outlets are capable of the loads required for your tools (especially if you have more than one item plugged in at a time). Turn off all electrical equipment after use.

- Always use tools and materials in accordance with the manufacturer's instructions.
- Store all liquid materials, such as paints and adhesives, in accordance with the manufacturer's instructions and away from any electrical outlets.
- Make sure your workspace is well ventilated, with at least one openable window.
- Always wear the correct safety equipment – such as face mask, gloves, goggles, aprons – for each stage of the project, for example goggles and mask for sanding, painting or using aerosols. Tie back long hair and remove scarves or loose garments that may get tangled in or contaminated by materials or equipment.
- Be aware of your posture. When working on miniatures you can lose track of time and end up standing or sitting in one position for long periods of time. Try to invest in a chair that is good for you and your posture. If standing or sitting for any length of time, take a break now and again and do some simple stretches or move about a little. You could even set a timer to remind you.
- Invest in a certified fire extinguisher – you can often find ones specifically for small areas such as caravans and workshops for around £20 – and make sure it is in date and is suitable for chemical/wood/paper/electrical fires.
- Be aware of your surroundings – make sure the floor is clear of cables and that doors are shut (to keep out pets or small children and keep in fumes and noise).
- Keep tools and equipment properly stored and maintained. If you have small children or pets, make sure any delicate or hazardous items are stowed safely out of reach. If you have a separate work area, keep it securely closed when not in use.
- Create a safety checklist for yourself and run through it when entering and leaving your workspace.

CHAPTER 2

SIMPLE CONSTRUCTION TECHNIQUES

This chapter begins with the fundamentals to get you started, before moving on to some slightly more advanced ones to widen your repertoire.

START SIMPLE

When first starting out making pieces using hand tools, opt for softer and thinner woods that are easier to cut and lighter for joining.

Choose simple shapes and styles. For example, one long rectangle with two smaller rectangles and two squares could make a chair; a table could be a rectangle with four or six straight legs with simple connectors between the legs. You can then add lathed legs or carved detailing to these designs with techniques you develop later.

Purchase two 1:12 scale dolls, one male adult (these are slightly taller than the female) and one child. These dolls will be your miniature-making buddy dolls that you can place next to or on your pieces as you make them to serve as a visual guide to whether your measurements are correct.

DEEP

. *Medium Balsa wood/Basswood/Plywood up to 4mm (4mm when cutting from both sides)*

. *Leather/Tooled Leather up to 4mm (possibly requiring cutting from both sides)*

. *Thicker Card*

. *Thick Fabric (Velvets/Cord etc)*

. *Medium Felt up to 3mm*

. *Polymer Clay*

. *Thin Foam*

. *Model-making Depron*

MEDIUM

. *Thin Balsa wood/Basswood/Plywood up to 3mm (3mm when cutting from both sides)*

. *Fabric (silk/cotton)*

. *Printable Fabric Sheets (cotton/Canvas etc)*

. *Thin Felt up to 2mm*

. *Medium Mylar*

. *Medium Acetate*

. *Medium Card*

. *Medium Vinyls*

STANDARD

. *Paper*

. *Thin Card*

. *Carbon Paper*

. *Thin Vinyls*

. *Thin Mylar*

. *Thin Acetate*

. *Tracing Paper*

. *Photo Paper*

. *Masking Materials/Tape*

Guide to craft blade uses.

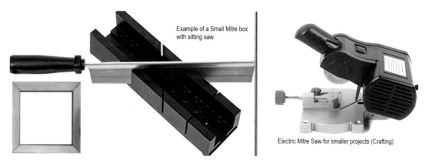

Mitre box with sitting saw and mini electric mitre saw.

Buy a small mitre block, specifically designed for small or miniature projects. This will enable you to cut accurate angled joins for picture frames, furniture top edgings, room skirting and so on. These are not expensive and can be found in most craft stores or online. You can also opt for a mini electric mitre/cutoff saw in order to save time and for larger miniature projects, such as flooring or ceiling pieces.

Joining Pieces

Always use the correct adhesives for your chosen materials. Wood glue will not hold metal pieces together. Some wood pieces that are simply stuck together may need the extra support of a nail or screw, or an angled join between the two pieces to strengthen the bond. Always read the manufacturer's instructions and follow safety guidelines. Take a note of the recommended drying times, as some adhesives will be fast drying, while others may take up to 24 hours or more. Always keep your drying pieces in a safe, dry and well-ventilated space that will remain undisturbed.

When joining pieces together by gluing or soldering, you should have one piece raised upon a support at the same height as the join to take the pressure off the join so that it can be worked upon easily.

Paper or medical tapes are useful to give joins that extra support whilst they set (for both metal and wood). Once the adhesive has completely dried, simply peel the tape off carefully and wipe or sand away any paper and glue residues.

When you are attaching printable fabrics and/or stripped tooled leather pieces, you will find it easier to line the back of your pieces with double-sided tape (like fabric or carpet tape) prior to cutting; this will mean that when you cut your piece, it will have complete adhesive coverage and it will also help to avoid any messy tape exposures.

Later you may wish to learn some construction techniques such as connecting pieces with hand-cut dovetail or square joints (*see* Further Reading). Dovetail joints are usually very strong, but applying a little wood glue within the joins before connecting (especially when you first start using this technique) is a good idea; again, ideally support the body of the piece while the glue is setting.

MORE ADVANCED TECHNIQUES

The lathe Again, start small with one you can practise on – a desk lathe for wood is a good choice (you can get lathes specifically for metal as well). You can either cut your own wood blanks (round or square columns) for your lathe or you can purchase them from wood suppliers or online. Always check the width and length of the wood pieces you are purchasing and, of course, the type of wood, as some are harder than others.

Carving/whittling Look for hand-carving tools or kits, which often come with a free eBook to get you started (or simply check out YouTube for free tutorials). This can be a lot of fun. Basswood (sometimes referred to as linden wood or lime wood) is a great wood for this as it is soft enough to carve by hand, yet hard enough to take small, detailed patterning.

Soldering Soldering is very simple, but you do need to be very careful to follow the manufacturer's safety instructions as you will be using very high temperatures. The area where you are working on your piece must be clear and appropriate for purpose (solder may drip) and you should wear appropriate safety clothing and mask.

Pyrography Writing with fire takes a bit of practice but the results can be truly stunning. Start with simple designs and strokes to get a feel for the tool you are using.

You can simply draw freehand on a piece of wood with the pyrography tool, but most people find it easier to use a pre-made design. There are several ways of transferring this onto your piece of wood. The simplest method is to use carbon paper, but this can be messy. Another way is to use the heated transfer tip that comes with your pyrography kit if you have one – it looks a little like a flat iron. Print off your design and attach it face down to a flat board using tape or clips. Then glide the transfer tip across the piece of paper in slow strokes until you have gone across the back of the whole image. The heat from the transfer tip will transfer the printer ink onto your piece of wood. You can now remove your transfer tip (using a pair of pliers, as it will be hot) and fit your chosen tip (usually pointy) instead and start tracing over the lines.

YouTube has a great many helpful tutorial videos on pyrography from starter to advanced level.

Leather tooling and embossing The projects in this book show how to use repurposed tooled leather items such as cigar boxes, belts, bags and so on, but there are some great starter kits you can buy to teach yourself how to tool leather, so you can emboss, bevel, stamp and carve to your own designs. Sites such as

Etsy often have wonderful leather-tooling presses and stamps for the more advanced, often with the option of commissioning leather stamps to your precise specifications.

LEAVING YOUR MARK

Throughout history, some furniture makers have left a distinct mark or signature item on their work, making each of their creations identifiable as one of their own. One such man was Robert Thompson – the Mouseman of Kilburn (a self-taught master of carving and joinery in oak). His beautiful handmade pieces often include a little carved mouse somewhere upon them and this is a tradition continued by Robert Thompsons Craftsmen Ltd in Yorkshire. You may choose to leave your own signature mark upon your miniature furniture pieces, whether it be your initials, a pattern a small carving.

One of Robert 'Mouseman' Thompson's trademark carvings. This one is on the altar rail in Kilburn parish church.

CHAPTER 3

FINISHING TECHNIQUES

This chapter will focus on finishing techniques you can use to give your miniatures an aged look or patina.

In Project 1 you will find explained in full the main painting and staining technique that will be used for many of the projects that come after it. You can alter this technique by using different shades and amounts of colour to achieve your desired outcome. The darker shades used throughout this book have been chosen to represent the darker woods often found in houses from medieval and Tudor times right through to the twentieth century. The stains, pens and sealant types are all also available in lighter wood tones, however, and in some cases can be found in a range of colours.

VARNISH AND SEALANT

Varnish, gloss and primer products are widely available on sites such as Amazon and eBay and at most DIY stores. When using any varnish, sealant or wood treatment materials, you should always follow the manufacturer's instructions and guidelines.

The main two-in-one wood sealant/varnish used throughout this book is by Contura (other brands include Ronseal, Rustins and The Army Painter).

It has a very runny, almost water consistency, which is easier to apply (thinly) and gives full and fast-drying coverage without leaving smears and droplets that can often occur with heavier fast-drying varnishes. Choose a colourless sealant/varnish, and always go for a solvent-free mix so that it falls into the child-safe category (often stated as saliva-proof); you are making collector's items here and not toys, but it is always wise to err on the side of caution. This type of two-in-one sealant/varnish is also great for maintenance, and giving your 1:12 scale pieces and dolls' houses an annual coat will keep them pristine and protected.

Make sure that any product you use for varnishing or painting has a recognised safety ISO/UFI standard upon it such as DIN EN (German Institute for Standardisation) and be aware of VOC content (volatile organic compounds) – always wear the appropriate protective clothing, including mask, goggles and gloves. UK and EU products should always have a UFI identification code (usually next to any warning messages), which helps to identify the chemical content should it be necessary to do so. Here are the names of just a few producers of varnish/sealant products – Ronseal, Rustins, Contura and The Army Painter (who also do a spray varnish for miniature/model making specifically for metal).

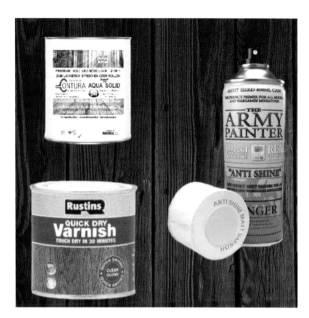

Contura two-in-one sealant and varnish, Rustins quick-drying clear gloss varnish and The Army Painter spray matt varnish.

TRANSFER STAINING

There are no absolute guarantees with wood sealants, and you will discover that even after sealing some pieces several times there can still be some staining where fabrics have come into contact with the wood. Keep this in mind when upholstering and wrapping any pieces that have been stained. You can opt to use darker fabrics to decorate and upholster items that have been stained or you can add a simple barrier between fabric pieces and the wood itself by cutting a small piece of card to place between the two. Alternatively, leave stained pieces to dry for much longer than the recommended time. This also applies when you are wrapping items to store or send in the post: to avoid unsightly contact staining on any wrapping materials, place items in a container first or wrap in a material that is either darker or disposable. The risk of contact transfer staining generally reduces over time.

AGING WOOD PIECES

Here some of the main methods and techniques to give miniature pieces an aged look:

Imitating dents and wear and tear Use a meat tenderiser to hit and add scratches and dents to pieces of wood; this will give a worn look to ceiling beams and wood panelling. Practise on some offcuts first to establish pressure and techniques.

Imitating wormholes Some old wood offcuts come with wormholes (residents long gone), which give a wonderful, aged look. If you want to add this look to your miniatures, you can simply use a very fine wood drill (either electric or manual) to make small shallow holes in your chosen wood before constructing the final piece. This look works well on 1:12 scale fireplaces and bedposts, for example. If you are a little nervous about the drill or concerned about splitting wood if the drill piece is not fine enough, you can make small holes using a small nail, tapped very lightly with a small hammer. It is easiest to add wormholes to flat wood pieces; carved items, such as bedposts, should be secured using a vice before drilling. Always do a test wormhole using an offcut of the actual type of wood your piece will be made from.

Cutting and sanding bare wood For wooden floorboards, ceiling beams, picture rails, skirting and furniture edging, you can simply use a craft knife to cut away some of the straight edges to give an aged effect. You can also cut into the wood slightly in random areas to give an uneven, worn feel. Look at actual ceiling beams online to see how pieces are not uniform, but often differ in thickness, colour and even quality. You can also simply rub down areas with sandpaper and/or wire wool to give an uneven effect.

Sanding painted wood Use medium to fine sanding sponges or sandpaper to rub down painted wood. A great effect can be achieved by lightly rubbing down corner areas and leg edges, especially when you have painted your miniatures with a contrasting undercoat, as you can rub down to different depths to reveal paint layers and even the bare wood in places. Real furniture often has paint scuffs and/or fading in areas that see a lot of use, such as the arms, legs, tabletops and seated areas, so these are the areas you should focus on.

Wood repair pens and stain Wood stain and wood repair pens are a perfect partnership and are widely available. The projects in the book are mainly completed using Tableau Wood Scratch Cover wood stain (dark wood) and standard furniture repair pens (which usually come in packs of five to eight different wood shades). Simply colour your wood – it does not have to be neat – with your chosen shade of repair pen; you can mix it up a bit by using more than one colour, as the stain will blend them. You can also use the black pen to colour areas that you may have cut away to give an uneven look, which will create a knotted wood effect area, or, in larger amounts, the appearance of dirt accumulation, for example around a fireplace or chimney. Once you have used your pens, simply coat with the wood stain. If you are not happy with the outcome, wait for piece to dry and then add more pen colour followed by the stain (this works on darker wood areas only).

Wax shoe polish This is perfect for instant aging and adding built-up areas of dirt or soot. You will need to experiment a little, using a lint-free cloth or a toothbrush to apply the polish. You can always scrape excess away if you apply too much, but wax polish is hard to remove completely, which makes it difficult if you then decide to paint the area instead (as the paint will not adhere to the waxed area); always test this method first on an offcut before applying to your finished piece.

Steel wool, vinegar and black tea Soak a piece of steel wool in some vinegar for at least 24 hours. Wipe down your piece of wood with boiled black tea using a paintbrush. Then apply the steel wool solution to your piece, again using a paintbrush. The vinegar reacts with the tea to give a darkened, aged effect. Allow the mixture time to dry and wipe away any residue with a damp cloth. You can then finish with a wax coating to seal the effect. Again, test this method on a small offcut of the same material before applying to your miniature.

Crackle glaze Paint your wood using an acrylic paint in your chosen colour. Once the paint has dried, apply white PVA glue generously over the whole area to give an opaque look, then leave it to dry a little until it feels tacky. Apply a second coat of paint (the same colour as before) to the tacky glue and allow it to dry – as it dries out, the cracks will appear. As with other methods, test the process first on a spare piece of wood of the same type that your miniature is made of.

AGING METAL PIECES

Most old metal pieces that you discover for repurposing will already come with some natural aging or damage, such as the gravy boat used in Project 9. To achieve a more aged or antique look, try one of the following methods.

Sanding sponges

Use these to rub down areas and expose differing tints and shades of metals. This works particularly well on many brass pieces, as often they are plated, and when rubbed down will expose a nickel or silver-coloured layer under the brass. Test a small area first, and always use a fine grade of paper or sponge, as you do not want to rub away any patterns or definition.

Brass

Apple vinegar and salt is great combination for aging brass. You will need a lidded plastic tub or old lidded drinks beaker (depending on the size of the piece) and protective clothing. Some people are sensitive to vinegar fumes, so wear a mask and goggles, and gloves so that you do not inadvertently rub your eyes with hands that have come into contact with the salt and vinegar, which can be highly acidic. For a piece approximately the size of a gravy boat, a tablespoon of salt and a tablespoon of vinegar will suffice; use about half this for small metal clock columns or finials.

Sanded brass exposing silver colour beneath.

1. Clean your metal piece first using a small brush or toothbrush.
2. Put the salt and apple vinegar into your container and make sure the salt has dissolved.
3. Put your metal piece into the container and brush the piece completely with the liquid, using a small paintbrush.
4. Turn the piece in the container to make sure it is covered in solution and then put the lid on.
5. Leave the sealed container for two or three hours and then rotate the item in the tub again.
6. After approximately four to eight hours, your metal should have darkened, and in places have a beautiful green patina. Leave it overnight in a safe place and then remove from the container and place onto some kitchen roll on your worktop and gently tap it dry.
7. Leave the treated brass to dry out overnight. The piece will continue to age.

Copper

Make sure to wear appropriate protective equipment including eye goggles, mask and gloves, as this process uses table salt, lemon juice, household ammonia and vinegar.

1. Start by cleaning the surface of your copper item with a commercial cleaner specifically for that purpose (trisodium phosphate).
2. Mix a small amount of ammonium chloride (ammonium chloride crystals are sold commercially as sal ammoniac) according to the manufacturer's instructions, and apply it to the copper surface using a small paintbrush. You will need roughly a tablespoon for a gravy boat-sized piece.
3. Make up a solution of one cup ammonia with water (as per manufacturer's instructions), one cup of table salt, one cup of lemon juice and one cup of vinegar and mix well.
4. Apply the solution to the cleaned metal surface.

Aged copper.

5. Put the piece to one side and allow the reaction to take place. A general guideline for reaction time is usually four to eight hours, so leaving overnight is a good way to achieve this without having to wait around. Meanwhile, dispose of any unused solution and tidy away leftover materials and used tools to a safe place. Throw away any disposable gloves used.

FINISHING WITH LEATHER

Tooled leather is perfect for covering wood pieces to give an antique carved wood look. There are many old items out there ideal for repurposing: belts, for example, can be perfect as bed side pieces and edgings, as well as fireplace surrounds (*see* Chapter 5). The picture here shows some examples of tooled leather items suitable for repurposing, including the old cigar box that will be used for the four-poster bed in Project 6. Such boxes can easily be found on sites such as eBay, at markets and car boot sales, and they are also great to use as wall panels or ceiling pieces. The thinner leathers can be used for upholstering chairs and so on. There are also a lot of old purses and handbags to be found that have tooled leather patterning; the close-up of a Medici design bag – the tan image in the middle of the picture – is the type of leather that can be repurposed to finish 1:12 scale pieces such as headboards and bench seats.

Always keep scale in mind when looking for tooled leather items. Belts are perfect as the patterning on belts is clearly designed to fit within a narrow width (around 2–5cm).

Usually, the tooled leather on boxes is easy to peel away from what is often a carboard backing. You can then simply cut the desired pieces with a craft knife and a standard ruler (use a safety ruler with finger guard). Belts can vary in thickness but are also very easy to cut with the same tools. Thicker leather belts can be thinned with a sharp leather-cutting knife, but this does require some practice.

Once you have successfully added the tooled leather, you can colour match it to your piece using the wood stain and wood pen finishing techniques covered earlier in this chapter.

Tooled leather belts, cigar boxes, frames, bags and jewellery boxes.

Wood veneer sheets.

DECORATIVE FINIALS

Finials help to enhance miniature pieces, and the suggestions given here should give you some idea of what to look for when sourcing your own materials.

Old jewellery, such as round, wooden-bead necklaces, are perfect as bedpost finials and even as furniture feet. Beads are used in this way in many of the projects covered in this book.

Old clock finials often come in wood, brass, silver or other metal. Some are truly beautiful, and you will find a variety of shapes, including cherubs, lions, medieval faces, acorns, Atlas holding the world – to name but a few. Look for broken clock cases and clock parts online (often these can include columns,

Examples of silver flatwire with a ruler to give an idea of scale.

which are perfect for miniature settings). The four-poster bed in the picture here was made almost completely from the repurposed wood, columns and finials from just one damaged clock.

Making your Own Finials

Making your own finials from scratch to your own unique design is deeply satisfying. Practise carving, whittling and using the lathe as much as possible so that you can achieve this at your own pace. Basswood (often referred to as linden wood or lime wood), mentioned in Chapter 2, is great for this purpose. You can progress to harder woods as you become more proficient in this skill. Again, you will benefit from watching training videos on social media sites such as YouTube, which are free and aimed at all levels.

You may even find that a certain design becomes your signature piece for your projects. Although it means investing time in making your own finials, you are not constrained as to when you make them.

A metal trim on wood can look beautiful, whether you choose silver, brass, copper, gold or bronze. There are many silversmiths and metal trim producers that offer trim work perfect for edging pieces of furniture. Sellers on platforms such as Etsy, eBay and Linktree

often advertise their supplies of metal trims (often known as flatwire) as being mainly for the purpose of jewellery making for rings or bracelets, and offer many antique-style patterns (including swirls, flowers, roman, murals, egg and dart, dot edge). These types of jewellery-making flatwire, ranging from about 3mm to 10mm in width, are perfect for 1:12 scale trims and edgings (including furniture and fireplaces). This size and type of flatwire is easy to bend and mould around curved edges and corners and can easily be fixed in place with adhesives

Four-poster bed made from a repurposed clock case.

CHAPTER 4

PROJECT 1: AGED PITCHED CEILING

This chapter presents the simplest project in this book. It is not actually a piece of furniture, but a basic pitched ceiling that uses some techniques that you can put into practice when making your own miniature furniture pieces. This project will also cover a few effective ways to give your wood furniture pieces an aged look.

TOOLS AND MATERIALS

1. Cutting mat – placed on a solid surface, ideally some sort of workbench or a secure and solid wooden board you can use as a worktop
2. Cardboard (enough for the area of ceiling you wish to cover)

Fig 1 Finished ceiling with printed apex.

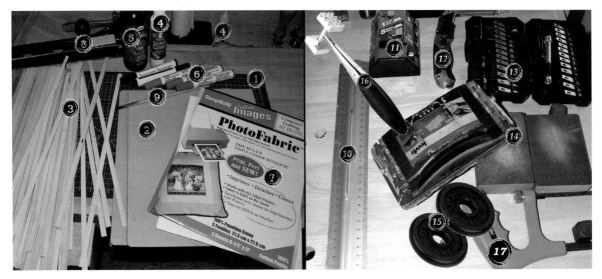

Fig 2 Workbench with all required tools and materials.

3. Bamboo crafting sticks, each 400mm × 9mm × 3mm
4. Adhesives – strong wood glue (Crocodile used here), industrial-grade superglue (Everbuild) and double-sided carpet tape
5. Dark wood stain – Tableau Scratch Cover used here
6. Furniture repair pens
7. Printable canvas fabric (optional) – Simplicity used here
8. Wood offcut – one piece for the central ceiling join
9. Small paintbrush
10. Metal ruler with finger guard
11. Spare blades for craft knife
12. Craft knife
13. Craft knife with spare blades (an alternative to the Stanley knife)
14. Hand sanding tool or sanding sponges
15 Dumbbell weights or heavy food or paint tins
16. Meat tenderiser with a pointed finish or a small hammer
17. Hand saw
18. Safety mask, goggles and gloves (not shown)
19. Workbench, ideally with vice or grip (not shown)

STEP-BY-STEP GUIDE

Making the Ceiling

1. Measure the internal ceiling space that needs to be covered and cut the card to size using a ruler and craft knife. Double-check the size is correct by slotting the card into the space. The ceiling in this example consists of two sloping sides running up to a central beam, so was made from two pieces of card.
2. Place the card (one piece at a time) on the cutting board. Stick pieces of bamboo to it side by side using wood glue. Once about eight pieces have been stuck down (the diameter of the dumbbell weight or heavy tin), stop and place the chosen weights on top of the glued pieces, making sure they are still positioned side by side (Fig 3). The weights will hold the bamboo in place whilst the glue sets.
3. Repeat the process until the whole sheet is covered with bamboo strips.
4. Trim the edges with a craft knife and ruler (wearing safety cutting gloves).
5. Cut some small nicks out of some of the bamboo strips and add small scratches with the craft knife. Gently hit some of the bamboo

Fig 3 Fix and weigh down the bamboo strips.

Fig 4 Fix the vertical sticks across the horizontal ones and weigh down, then trim the edges.

Fig 5 Colour and stain to the desired outcome – a block of colour, patchy or mixed.

with the meat tenderiser to give a time-worn effect. Leave some of the strips intact in areas, for example near the doors or end walls – on real ceiling beams, areas are often more worn by the windows (light and weather damage) and above fireplaces. If any of the bamboo pieces appear to be loose, then simply re-glue and weight down.

6. Give the sheet a gentle rub down (not too much, otherwise the worn/damaged effects will be rubbed away).

7. Add bamboo strips in the other direction with a gap of approximately 4cm between each strip. Weigh the glued pieces down again with the weights. Once the strips are dry, repeat step 5 to create a worn affect. Trim the edges as in step 3.

8. Colour the bamboo using the scratch repair pens (starting unevenly and building up colour until the desired look is achieved). Use the black scratch repair pen to add darker sections in areas where there is shade and above the fireplace. One option is to apply a solid block of colour with some darker blackened areas added (as in the middle three sections in Fig 5); alternatively, go for a patchy look or a solid look in a lighter colour. It is always possible to add darker areas later by repeating the process when the piece is dry. Another option is to add a little wax black boot polish above

fireplace areas or on fireplace backplates (wood ones or matt brick tiles) to add a scorched look.

9. Glue the pieces of card to the ceiling with wood glue, using some leftover bamboo sticks to hold them in place while they dry. Leave for a few days to fix. Check that all pieces are firmly in place before removing the supporting bamboo sticks.

10. Choose the piece of wood for the ceiling central beam (which will join the sloping ceiling pieces). Add some damage or worn effects as in step 5 if desired. Rub down and treat with scratch repair pens and wood stain to match the earlier pieces.

11. Fix the central beam in place and add some bamboo lengths to support the piece while the glue fixes, as for the ceiling pieces in step 9 (Fig 6).

WORMHOLES

Adding wormholes to wood beams can give an extra-aged appearance. This works particularly well with the harder woods. Use a manual hand drill with a superfine wood drill piece to create random clusters of holes (test on an offcut first to get used to the pressure – these superfine drill pieces can break easily). Then add a touch of wood stain to each hole to give a natural appearance.

Fig 6 Excess bamboo sticks holding the ceiling piece in place.

Leave for a few days and check that the beam is securely fixed in place before removing the support sticks.

Decorated Apex

Adding a painted canvas in the apex at one end is an optional finishing touch.

12. Choose the desired image, pattern or painting to add to your ceiling wall/apex space. The image used in this example was a copy of an original Renaissance print purchased on Etsy (Fig 7).

13. Measure and draw a template of the space to be filled (in this case it was a triangular apex) and cut out a piece of card to fill the area. Print a copy of the chosen image at the same size onto the printable canvas for a real painted effect. Some small oil paint additions will enhance the look.

14. Now attach the printed canvas to the cut-to-size card piece using double-sided carpet tape and then glue the piece into the apex space using industrial-strength superglue.

Fig 7 Choose an image to match your chosen theme for the apex.

15. Tidy up any exposed edges or joins using the same bamboo strips as for ceiling pieces. Colour them first, either the same colour as the ceiling or in a contrast shade – black in this example. It is important to seal these stained bamboo strips before placing over the exposed edges to avoid contact staining; alternatively, create a barrier between the two by adding a thin card strip to the side of the bamboo strip that will touch the canvas. Gently fix the strips in place and, if necessary, hold them using bamboo sticks as for the ceiling pieces.

This simple ceiling design can easily be embellished with your own carved or patterned trims or edges and cross beams and support beams.

In this example, no sealant or varnish has been applied to the ceiling, but it can be added later if required. Furthermore, these stained pieces will continue to age over time, and it is likely that eventually some of the darker pen colours will start to show through; more staining can be added to deal with this, or to match any wall panelling or floors. It is a good idea to wait a month or two before applying extra wood stain or any varnish/sealant, to see how the piece ages.

CHAPTER 5

PROJECT 2: FIREPLACE

This project for an antique-look fireplace makes use of both handmade and repurposed materials. The measurements given are suitable for a medium to large 1:12 scale fireplace. The dimensions can be increased or reduced, depending on the materials used and the setting the fireplace is intended for, but always bear in mind that the scale of any patterning should match – a larger-scale patterning on a pressed tin piece will look odd. Identifying pieces for repurposing into a 1:12 scale setting is not an exact science, but over time you will be able to spot these pieces easily. As a general rule, for a fireplace, front sides 2–3.5cm wide fit well in a 1:12 scale setting, with the length varying according to design.

This project shows a piece made with craft wood and bamboo, which are easy to source and simply require cutting (no carving or lathe skills), but of course you can add your own patterned or carved edgings and finials, or use different materials or wood types (keeping an eye on thickness if cutting by hand).

Fig 1 Fireplace with fireguard.

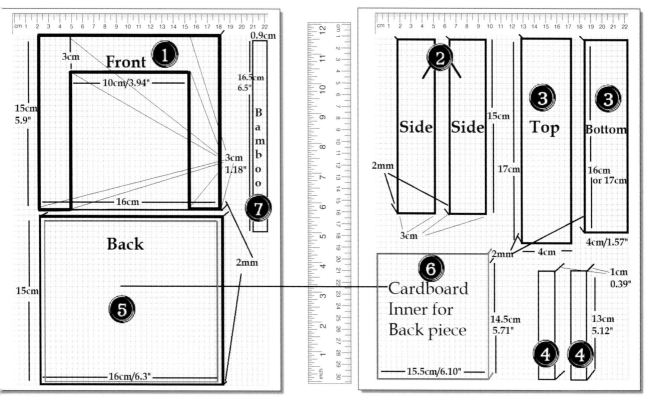

Fig 2 Fireplace plan.

FIREPLACES THROUGH THE AGES

Fireplaces come in all shapes and sizes with some being simply decorated and others being a central focus to a room. Tudor halls and kitchens often had huge, stone walk-in fireplaces that could be plain or heavily carved. The Georgian fireplace was often also heavily carved in stone, marble or wood, with classically styled side columns. Some small Victorian fireplaces were made of cast iron, and bedrooms would have smaller fireplaces (possibly in a corner setting) that often incorporated cast iron elements. Towards the end of the Victorian period, the fireplace took on new, uncomplicated stylistic features, with tiles and simple patterns becoming popular in Edwardian times.

By the nineteenth century and beyond, styles and materials from different periods were often combined, and this can make it more difficult to differentiate a Victorian fireplace from a Georgian one, for example. The key point is to keep in mind the materials that were available in any given period and how those materials could be tooled.

TOOLS AND MATERIALS

1. Two basswood sheets – each approximately 250mm × 390mm × 2mm (which leaves plenty spare for errors and future projects), for wood pieces nos 1, 2, 3 and 5. To buy the exact size of craft wood required, measure the area needed for all the pieces and add together
2. Selection of edging/finials – used here are bamboo strips (9mm wide × 3mm thick for piece no. 7) and bamboo skewer sticks for edging the tooled leather
3. Mixed tooled leather – from old leather frames, cigar boxes, trinket boxes and so on. When searching for tooled leather for repurposing, always keep in mind the pattern sizing. A belt may need to be thinned with a skiving knife
4. Pressed tin trinket or cigarette box – the one used for this project is 11.5cm × 9cm (lid) and 5cm tall (base)

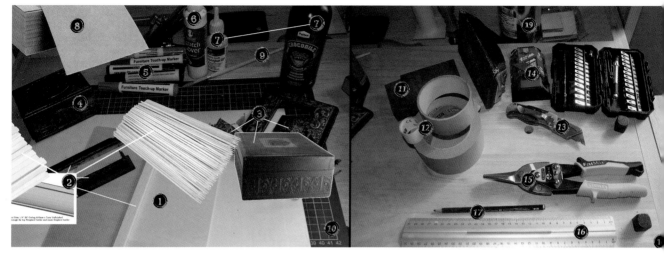

Fig 3 Workbench with all required tools and materials.

5. Wood furniture markers; for this project, mainly darker pens, such as mahogany and black, were used
6. Dark wood stain – Tableau Scratch Cover in Dark used here
7. Adhesives – industrial-grade superglue (Everbuild used here) and strong wood glue (Crocodile)
8. Cardboard – one piece of A5 card, 2mm thick
9. Small paintbrush
10. Cutting mat – placed on a solid surface, ideally some sort of workbench or secure and solid wooden board used as a worktop
11. Sanding sponge or hand sander – coarse wet and dry for wood
12. Tapes – Tesa paper tape, 3M medical tape and strong double-sided tape
13. Craft knife
14. Spare blades for the craft knife
15. Metal cutter/snipper tool with safety – the one used here is a Stanley FatMax
16. Ruler with finger guard
17. Pencil
18. Workbench or secure worktop area
19. Two-in-one varnish and sealant – Contura Aqua Solid used here
20. Safety mask, goggles and gloves (not shown)

STEP-BY-STEP GUIDE

Preparing the Pressed Tin

There are many videos on YouTube about tin-cutting methods. Always practise on a scrap piece of the tin before cutting the main area you wish to use, especially when using what may be a one-of-a-kind piece, or one that took a long time to source.

1. Wearing cut-proof safety gloves, use the metal cutter to cut out the pieces of tin (from the sourced tin piece) for the backplate and fireguard (Fig 4). The number and shape of the pieces will depend on the design and size of the tin source; for this piece, the lid was used (simply removed, not cut) along with the front piece for the main backplate, and then the remaining back and side pieces were used for the fireguard.

Fig 4 Cutting pieces of tin.

Be extra careful when cutting out the fireguard shape, as the metal edges can be sharp. Cut as with scissors and paper, but slowly and with extra pressure. Where there are straight lines to be cut, snip vertically down to each side of the line and attempt to fold the metal back and forth along the line until the piece comes away by itself (this will only work if the metal is thin enough; otherwise it will need to be cut).

2. Remove any sharp edges (cut and sand). For the backplate, the edges will be hidden behind the fireplace main frame, so this needs to be done simply for safety during construction rather than for aesthetics.

3. Still wearing cut-proof gloves (as metal edges can still be a hazard), clean the tin pieces with a soft sanding sponge and some soapy water; more stubborn dirt can be shifted with bicarbonate of soda or simply toothpaste applied with a toothbrush. The backplate can be highly polished or left dirty for a used look, depending on the desired effect. When the tin is clean, leave it to dry and rinse the gloves.

4. Now focus on your backplate. If more than one piece is needed for this, they will need to be joined together with industrial-strength superglue. Paper tape can be useful to add extra support while the glue is drying. If pieces have different edges (in this example, where the lid piece rim is joined to the cut edge), simply cut a thin piece of wood and glue to the back of the flat piece to create an area that can by glued and joined to the rimmed piece (Fig 5).

Wood Strip

Fig 5 Creating a firm join using a strip of wood glued to back of the piece.

Preparing the Wood Pieces

5. Using Fig 2 as a guide, measure and mark each piece of wood ready for cutting.
6. Label each piece using some 3M tape and a pen.
7. Place the marked-out wood sheets onto the cutting mat. Cut the pieces out using a craft knife, and sand down any rough edges (Fig 6).

Preparing the Tooled Leather

8. Strip the tooled leather from the source piece (for example cigar box, trinket box) using a sharp craft knife and a ruler. Cut a bold line around the edge of the area to be removed and then gently peel back a thin layer from below the actual leather surface (usually a cardboard layer) until the section is removed from the rest of the card.
9. Cover the back of the tooled leather with strong double-sided tape (for paper or fabric).

Fig 7 Preparing the tooled leather prior to cutting.

10. Cut the leather to the required size using a ruler and craft knife. Depending on the volume of tooled leather and the design, it may not be possible to cover the wood with one piece; in that case, several pieces can be joined together.
11. Once the leather has been cut to size, peel back the tape and stick it to wood piece no. 1. If only part of the wood has been covered, it is a good idea to edge the piece to give a finished look. The piece here was edged with bamboo skewer sticks cut to size and fixed using the wood glue (wipe away any residue).

Assembly

12. Glue side pieces no. 2 to the back of front piece no. 1. Use a square block (sanding sponges used here) to hold the sides in position while the glue dries (Fig 10). Once the glue is dry, add another layer of glue to the internal joins and leave to dry again.
13. Fix the no. 4 pieces to the back of the no. 1 piece with wood glue, as shown in Fig 11. Leave to dry.
14. Using the double-sided sticky tape, attach card no. 6 to the centre of back piece no. 5.
15. Add a thin layer of superglue to the outer edges of the no. 2 side pieces and then fix the

Fig 6 Draw the required pieces out on the wood sheets, cut and sand.

Fig 8 Two examples of tooled leather fireplaces using the same plan but with slightly differing finishes.

Fig 9 Attaching the tooled leather onto the front piece.

back piece no. 5 in place (with a cardboard piece on the inside of the fireplace). Hold for a couple a few minutes until secure. Turn the piece over and add a layer of wood glue to the internal joins between the back piece and side pieces using a cotton bud. Leave to dry.

16. Turn the piece over to look into the fireplace. Add a layer of wood glue to the top outer edges of the piece and fix the top piece no. 4.

17. Apply a layer of superglue to the back of the tin backplate piece prepared in step 4 and slide it up between the no. 4 pieces and fix it centrally onto the cardboard on the back piece.

Fig 10 Attaching the side pieces.

Fig 11 Attaching fireplace inner edges (ignore the cardboard added to top here).

Fig 12 The top, inner tin backplate, bottom and wood trim all fitted.

18. Fix the bottom piece in place, either cut to the same size as the top or to fit with the edges.
19. Fix wood strip/bamboo piece no. 7 in place with wood glue. Hold the pieces in place while they are drying.
20. Once all the separate pieces are fixed in place and all glue is dry, check the whole piece for rough or uneven edges, and rub down accordingly.

Colouring and Staining

21. Add a solid block of colour using the wood touch-up markers in the desired shade. This piece was mostly finished in black, but in places oak and mahogany shades were put down underneath the black, and these tones will come through over time.
22. Apply a coat of wood scratch repair to the wood.
23. It is an option at this point to add a small amount of wood stain to the tooled leather (either all over or just in parts) to get a more matched look between the wood and leather. Before doing this, test it on a spot of leather first in case it goes too dark, which may obscure any patterning; keep in mind, however, that wood and tooled leather will both appear darker while the wood stain is still wet.
24. Allow to dry overnight.
25. Touch up any missed or sub-standard areas.
26. Once any touched-up areas are dry, simply seal and/or varnish.

Fireguard and Finials

27. The optional fireguard can be made very simply and quickly using the last piece of the pressed tin. Cut out around the shaped area (Fig 13).

28 Clean this piece using the same method as for the backplate in step 3.

29. Cover any sharp/exposed edges with small cut pieces of bamboo stick. Here the sticks were painted black prior to cutting. A small, curved piece was cut out of 2mm basswood to fix to the back of the patterned front area (again painted black).

30. To finish, add some small beads, and, if necessary, a base strip of wood to support and balance the piece.

The fireguard can also be made and added later if desired. Fig 14 shows the fireplace with fireguard in a 1:12 scale setting.

Finials (not fitted in this example) are another optional extra. Simply add a thin wood support backing to the cut tin piece and frame with fine-cut finials (using painted wood or card) to give a more sophisticated look. It would also be possible to add corbels to support the fireplace top, or shelving or a fitted frame/chimney area to the top piece.

Fig 13 Cut around the outline of the design.

Fig 14 The fireplace in its 1:12 scale setting.

CHAPTER 6

PROJECT 3: SIMPLE TABLE

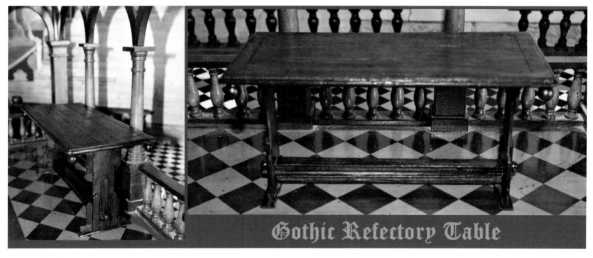

Fig 1 Gothic refectory table: side and end view.

The table in this project is a long Gothic refectory table based on an original pencil sketch (Fig 3). It can be made using simple hand tools and materials that can be purchased easily from any good craft store or online.

This table is a little longer than a usual kitchen table, which is normal for a refectory table. In fact, it could be even longer to fill a long hall or shorter to make a side table; simply adjust the length of the tabletop, table underpiece and any edgings accordingly.

Bare wood has been used here to clearly show the construction and how to colour the piece. Of course,

you could use another type of wood instead or cover the piece in sheets of veneer, for example oak or walnut.

Depending on your skill level, you can also incorporate your own design elements in this piece, for example by adding carved ends to reflect the original (Fig 3) – you will need to use a thicker piece of wood for this and account for it when cutting the tabletop underpiece no. 2. You could also draw on Gothic arch patterns prior to assembly using pyrography. This and other embellishments can also be added later.

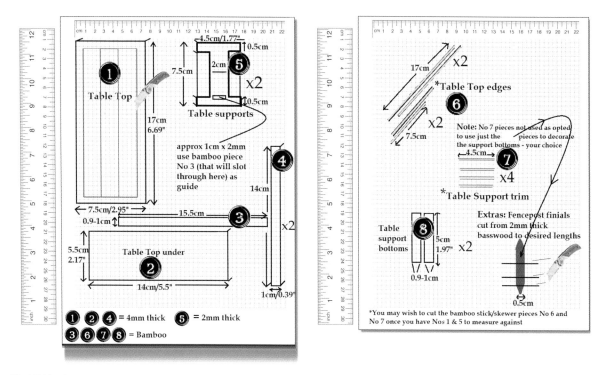

Fig 2 Table plan.

Fig 3 Sketch of the original Gothic refectory table with carved ends.

TOOLS AND MATERIALS

1. Mixed wood veneer sheets, in a mix of 2mm and 4mm thicknesses (optional)
2. One pine wood panel sheet – approximately 250mm × 390mm × 4mm for pieces 1, 2 and 4; one basswood sheet – approximately 200mm × 200mm × 2mm, more than enough for the no. 5 pieces and optional fence post pieces
3. One bamboo strip, 400mm × 9mm × 3mm
4. Thin bamboo skewers; optionally also thick bamboo sticks for edging
5. Wood beads, 4mm and 2mm diameter
6. Furniture repair pens
7. Decorlack acrylic paint in Glossy Black
8. Strong wood glue – Crocodile used here
9. Industrial-grade superglue – Everbuild HV used here (this is the thicker gel type, as opposed to the fluid version, and is less prone to dripping and being absorbed too deeply by the wood)
10. Two-in-one wood sealant and varnish – Contura used here
11. Dark wood stain – Tableau Scratch Cover in Dark used here
12. Paintbrush
13. Cutting mat
14. Fencepost pieces (optional) – these were pre-cut and edge stained from a prior project, but are simply cut from a 2mm thick basswood sheet
15. Craft knife and spare cutting blades
16. Tapes – Tesa paper tape and 3M medical tape
17. Sanding sponges or hand sander – coarse wet and dry for wood
18. Metal ruler with finger guard
19. Workbench or secure worktop
20. Safety mask, goggles and gloves (not shown)

Fig 4 Workbench with all required tools and materials.

STEP-BY-STEP GUIDE

Scoring blank sheets of basswood with a craft knife is a simple way to create plank-like pieces that really show once the piece is coloured and stained (as with the tabletop shown on the left in Fig 1). Press the blade firmly enough to create the mark (as when drawing) but not hard enough to actually cut more than a third of the way into the chosen wood sheet.

1. Using Fig 2 as a guide, measure and mark each piece of wood ready for cutting. On pieces over 2mm thick, mark the area to be cut on both sides of the wood (pieces 1, 2 and 4). When cutting the no. 5 pieces, take extra care when cutting the small 10mm × 2mm slot. After drawing the slot, cut carefully with a push and rocking motion until the lines are cut (to prevent any breakage in this delicate area); use bamboo piece no. 3 to check that it will slot through here.

2. Label each piece using some 3M tape and a pen, and place the pieces on the cutting mat (Fig 5).

3. Cut out the pieces using a craft knife and ruler. Leave the labels in place. Sand smooth any rough edges using a sanding block or sponge.

4. Use a craft knife to mark out a rectangle and two vertical lines inside it on the tabletop piece (Fig 6). This does not have to be 100 per cent accurate as we are trying to recreate an aged piece where the planks would not have looked exactly the same.

5. At this stage, add scratches or chips to the tabletop piece to enhance the aged look if desired. Use the craft knife to add light scratches and to cut out some slight notches on the edge of tabletop. Bear in mind that scratches will come through darker if wood stain is applied later.

Fig 5 Draw out the required pieces on the wood sheets, cut out and label.

Fig 6 Mark the tabletop to resemble a planked piece.

6. Stick the no. 6 bamboo pieces into place around the tabletop edge with wood glue (Fig 7). Wipe away any excess glue with a cotton bud or lint-free cloth before securing the bamboo in place with some strips of 3M or paper tape. Wait for piece to dry.

7. Once the bamboo edging is completely dry, remove the tape and gently rub down the bamboo edging to the desired finish (smooth, rough or thinner in some areas). Sanding the corner edges will give a slight curve finish.

8. Stick the no. 2 wood pieces to the centre of the underside of tabletop piece no. 1 with wood glue (Fig 8).

9. Glue the side pieces into place as shown in Fig 9, against the newly fitted underside piece and the area of the tabletop connection. Use sanding sponges, or something similar in shape and size, to support the side pieces while they dry.

10. Thread through bamboo piece no. 3 to line up the two side pieces opposite each other (Fig 9).

11. Making sure that the no. 3 bamboo piece is centrally positioned, with equal amounts slotted through each side, add a thin layer of superglue to one side, and both ends of the no. 4 pieces. Gently fix one of the no. 4 pieces (glue side

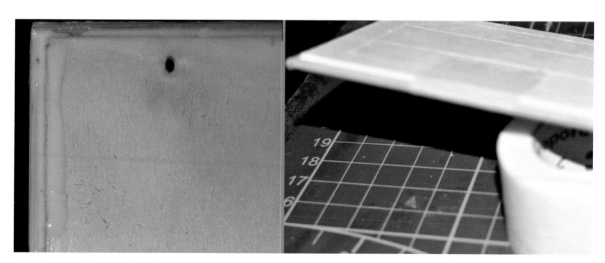

Fig 7 Edge the tabletop with bamboo sticks.

Fig 8 Fixing the underside of the tabletop.

Fig 9 Fixing the side pieces against the underside edge and tabletop.

Fig 10 Fixing the central stretcher in place to give support to the table.

down) onto one side of the no. 3 bamboo piece, and the other to the other side (Fig 10).

12. Fix the no. 8 bamboo pieces to the bottoms of each side piece and stand in an upright position to dry.

13. At this point, add any finials, carvings or decorated pieces. Fig 3 is a sketch of an original Gothic refectory table with a detail of the carved side. For simplicity, this example uses fencepost-shaped pieces with added bead finials.

14. The piece is now ready to be coloured, stained or varnished. Like the other pieces in this book, the finish here is a dark wood effect. Start by using wood corrector pens to add a solid block of colour to the whole piece. Use some black to create stained areas in the wood to give a natural appearance (Fig 11).

15. Stain the piece with the desired wood stain; Tableau Scratch Cover Dark wood stain has been used here. Leave the stain to dry overnight. At this point the marked plank pieces should start to appear.

16. Apply Decorlack carefully to any areas that the wood stain did not adhere to (for example areas that are hard to access or that may have had some remaining glue residue on them) and to places that would naturally have become darker over time, such as corners and edges.

17. Once the table is completely dry, add a coat of wood seal/varnish to give added protection and seal in the colour.

Fig 11 Colouring and staining.

CHAPTER 7

PROJECT 4: TUDOR BOX CHAIR

This project, creating a high-back Tudor box chair, leads nicely into the Tudor bench piece in Project 5. The design is represented at a level that is achievable by all levels of miniature maker, although, as with previous pieces, it can be improved with additional embellishments such as carved arms or decorative finials.

The sizes given for 2mm and 4mm wood sheets are a little larger than is strictly necessary, allowing for errors as well as finials and possible extra pieces.

TOOLS AND MATERIALS

1. One pine wood panel sheet – approximately 250mm × 390mm × 4mm for pieces nos 1 and 3
2. One basswood sheet – approximately 200mm × 200mm × 2mm, enough for all the 2mm-thick pieces
3. Strong wood glue – Crocodile was used here
4. Dark wood stain and furniture scratch repair pens – used here was Tableau Scratch Cover in Dark
5. Two-in-one wood sealant and varnish – Contura used here
6. Bamboo skewer sticks
7. Four bamboo strips, each 400mm × 9mm × 3mm
8. Industrial-grade superglue
9. Cutting mat, placed on a solid surface, ideally a workbench or secure and solid wooden board used as a worktop
10. Tapes – Tesa paper tape and 3M medical tape
11. Sanding sponges or hand sander – coarse wet and dry for wood
12. Craft knife
13. Spare cutting blades

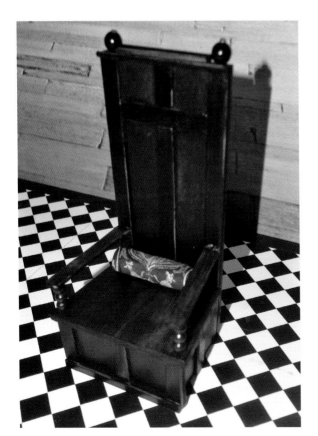
Fig 1 A high-backed Tudor box chair.

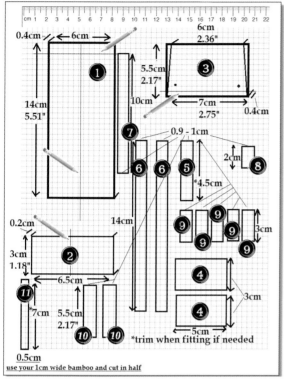

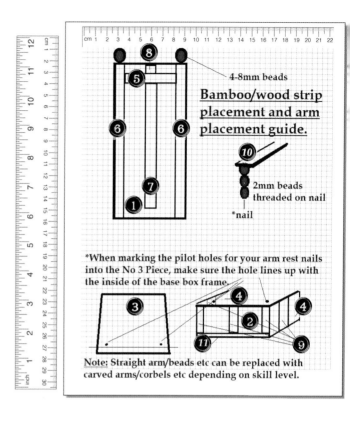

Fig 2 Plan for the box chair.

Fig 3 Workbench with all required tools and materials.

14. Small hammer

15. Small wood nails

16. Ruler with finger guard

17. Pencil

18. Selection of finials (personal choice)

19. Sharp craft scissors

20. Workbench or secure worktop

21. Safety mask, goggles and gloves (not shown)

When first attempting to make a new piece of furniture, it is always a good idea to do a dry run of each of the main construction stages. For this piece that would be the back piece and the base piece. Follow the plan and the steps without using any glue (holding the pieces together with tape only). Once you are satisfied that everything fits, go back and follow the steps again, this time with wood glue. This approach will take you a little longer, but what you lose in time, you gain in confidence.

STEP-BY-STEP GUIDE

1. Using Fig 2 as a guide, measure and mark each piece of wood ready for cutting. For pieces over 2mm thick (nos 1 and 3), mark the area to be cut on both sides.
2. Label each piece using some 3M tape and a pen (Fig 4).
3. Place the marked-out wood sheets onto the cutting mat. Cut out the pieces with a craft knife and ruler; here a Stanley-type knife was used for the 4mm and 2mm pieces, and a finer craft knife for the thinner woods.

Leave the labels in place. Pieces 1 and 3 will need to be cut from both sides of the wood, as the 4mm thickness requires a little more effort to achieve an even cut without using electric tools.
4. Gently sand any rough edges using sanding block or sponge.

Back Piece

5. Draw a 14cm line down the centre of the no. 1 back piece, then a horizontal line 2cm from the top.
6. Fix bamboo strips to the back piece with wood glue (Fig 5).
7. Leave to dry for at least two hours. If necessary, put a heavy weight on top of any pieces not lying flat.
8. Once the back piece is dry, rub down any edges that need tidying or lining up.

Box Chair Base

9. Draw a horizontal line 5mm from the top (longest side) of the no. 3 wood piece.
10. Apply a thin layer of glue to the long outer edge of piece no. 2 and fix it to the drawn line on no 3.

Fig 4 Mark and label the wood pieces ready for cutting.

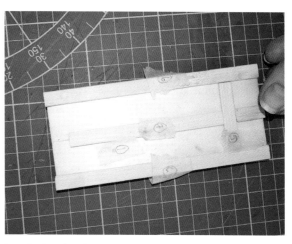

Fig 5 Sticking bamboo strips on the back piece.

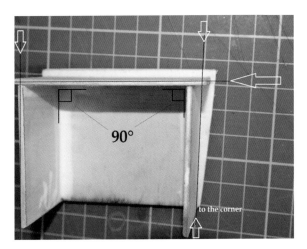

Fig 6 Main box-seat base structure.

Fig 7 Joining the back piece to the seat.

11. Attach both no. 4 pieces (Fig 6).

12. Apply a layer of glue to the joins on the inside of the base and use a cotton bud or thin scrap of cloth to wipe away any residue.

13. If necessary, stick paper or medical tape round the pieces to add additional support while they dry.

Assembly

14. Once the main box seat is structure is dry, it is time to add the no. 9 pieces. Draw a line down the centre of each of the base front and side pieces. Fix three of the no. 9 pieces to the no. 2 piece (one to each side edge and one in the middle) and then one to the middle of each of the no. 4 side pieces (Fig 7).

15. The main box seat base can now be attached to the back piece. Apply glue to the outer edges of the main box seat piece that will touch the back piece. Use a support to push against the back piece while this connection dries, and leave it to dry for at least two hours.

16. Add the no. 11 piece by applying wood glue to the bottom edge areas of the base where it will

rest against the previously fixed no. 9 pieces. Allow to dry in place.

17. Once the glue has dried, gently turn the piece over and add a layer of glue to the internal joins between the back and base piece. Wipe away any residue and leave to dry as before.

Arms

18. Using a wood puncture tool or a Stanley knife, mark a dot between 5mm and 10mm in from each front corner of the no. 3 pieces. This is where the nail with the threaded beads (*see* step 19) will go for the arm support on each side of the chair, so it is important to ensure that the dot falls within the internal area of the under-base frame (to avoid nail exposure on the outside). Dots marked in error can be sanded away later.

19. Thread three small 2mm wood beads onto a thin 2cm-long nail and gently hammer it into one of the scored holes; repeat on each side (Fig 8). The no. 10 arm pieces can now be attached.

Fig 8 Beading and attaching the armrest supports.

Apply a spot of superglue to the top of each nail and a thin strip of wood glue to one short end of each arm.

20. Press and hold each arm in place as shown in Fig 9, with the glued edge touching the base back approximately 2cm from the seat. Hold each arm in place for about two minutes.

Colouring, Staining and Sealing

21. Add any decorative wooden pieces, such as finials, at this stage so that they get the same colour treatment as the main frame of the piece. In this example, two 8mm wood beads were added to the top of each side of the back piece (using a small nail) before staining.

22. Colour the piece with the desired shade of wood scratch repair pen and wood stain. Make sure the chair is completely covered in pen before staining (Fig 10). Be careful when colouring the arms and the edge joins (use just the tip of the pens), as these are quite delicate.

23. Wood stain takes a while to dry, so leave the piece at least overnight (check manufacturer's

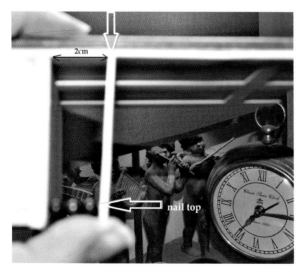

Fig 9 Adding the chair arms.

Fig 10 Colouring the chair.

instructions). Once it is dry, add another coat if necessary to cover any missed areas.

Finials

24. To give a slightly edged look, attach two 8mm wood beads to the top of the piece and then cut to size two no. 6 pieces to place between the two beads. Project 5 also offers some suggestions for simple finial ideas that could be applied here.

No upholstery or fixed fabrics were used in this project, but a removable bolster cushion has been added, helping to tie it to the bench in the next project and showing how simple touches can create set pieces (Fig 11).

Fig 11 Match up different pieces by using the same upholstery.

MEDICI CARRIAGE

Fifteenth-century Italy saw the noble Medici family thrive. They were affluent as a result of the success of their banking business, which gave them great political influence as well. Their position in society meant they owned some of the most beautiful buildings and furniture of this period. This carriage is based upon an original carriage from this period that was found in Italy and restored to be used in the miniseries *The Medici*. The methods used to make it are essentially an extension of the Tudor chair and Tudor bench designs.

Fifteenth-century Medici carriage in 1:12 scale.

CHAPTER 8

PROJECT 5: TUDOR BENCH

This chapter presents a project for a Tudor bench seat with high back. This is a piece that certainly would benefit from dovetail joins for the base, but for simplicity the instructions use wood glue, making the project accessible to all skill levels. This piece can be a bit fiddly, but persevere – any messy glue joins can be tidied up later with cotton buds or a gentle rub-down.

You can measure each of the areas that need to be cut (from 2mm and 4mm thickness) and cut your own woods, or purchase supplies that more exactly match the volume required. Either way, it is a good idea to have a little more wood than is required to allow for errors or additions. Any offcuts can be used for future projects.

Fig 1 shows examples of the bench seat back in two different finishes.

Fig 1 Tudor bench with two different finishes.

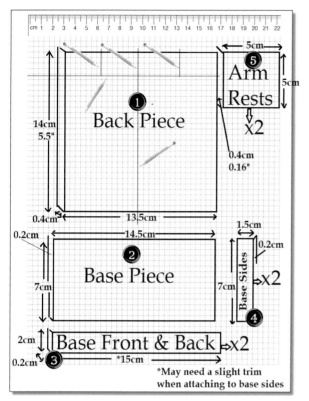

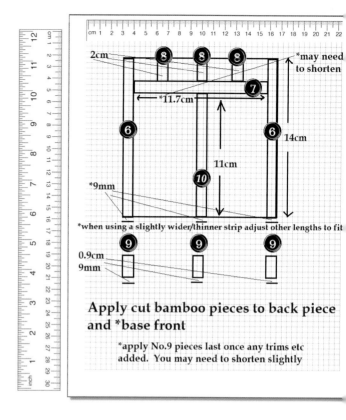

Fig 2 Tudor bench plan.

TOOLS AND MATERIALS

1. One pine wood panel sheet, approximately 250mm × 390mm × 4mm, which is more than enough for pieces 1 and 5

2. One basswood sheet, approximately 200mm × 200mm × 2mm, enough for pieces 2, 3 and 4

3. Strong wood glue – Crocodile used here

4. Dark wood stain – Tableau Scratch Cover in Dark used here

5. One A4 sheet of solid cardboard (not corrugated), approximately 2mm thick – cardboard from an old broken A4 folder was used here

Fig 3 Workbench with all required tools and materials.

6. Four bamboo strips, each 400mm × 9mm × 3mm
7. Furniture repair pens
8. Cutting mat, placed on a solid surface, ideally a workbench or secure and solid wooden board used as a worktop
9. Workbench or solid and secure worktop
10. Metal ruler with finger guard
11. Sanding sponges or hand sander – coarse wet and dry for wood
12. Craft knife, such as Rolson or Stanley
13. Spare cutting blades
14. Sharp craft scissors for card
15. Selection of finials in wood and silver, such as old beads, necklace parts and miniature offcuts
16. Small paintbrush
17. Mixed fabrics, such as old ties and velvet offcuts with some miniature tassels, and bolster kit
18. Tapes – Tesa paper tape, 3M medical tape, strong double-sided tape and double-sided fabric tape; if the last is not available, use the strong double-sided tape instead
19. Small wood nails with hammer (not shown)
20. Safety mask, goggles and gloves (not shown)

STEP-BY-STEP GUIDE

As suggested for the Tudor chair piece in the previous project, it is a good idea to attempt a dry run for this piece before applying the wood glue (using just paper or medical tape). Put the pieces together using the image of the complete piece in Fig 1 and the steps below.

1. Using Fig 2 as a guide, measure and mark each piece of wood ready for cutting. Pieces of wood that are over 2mm thick (nos 1 and 5) will need to be marked on both sides.
2. Label each piece using some 3M tape and a pen.
3. Place pieces 1–10 on the cutting mat (Fig 4).
4. Cut out these pieces using a knife and ruler. Start with Stanley- or Rolson-type knife for the 4mm and 2 mm pieces and switch to a finer craft knife for thinner woods. Leave the labels on.
5. Pieces 1 and 5 will need to be cut from both sides of the wood as the 4mm thickness requires a little more effort to achieve an even cut.
6. Smooth any rough edges using a sanding block or sponge.

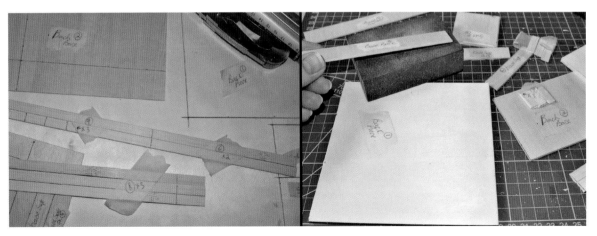

Fig 4 Draw out the required pieces on the wood sheet, cut out and sand.

Fixing Bamboo Strips to the Back Piece

7. Take the back piece and mark a line down the centre longways. Then mark a line across the width of the piece 2cm from the top (Fig 2 left).

8. Apply wood glue to the no. 6 pieces and attach to each inside edge of the no. 1 back piece (Fig 2, right).

9. Apply wood glue to one side of piece no. 7 and fix between the two outer no. 6 pieces with the top level with the pre-drawn line 2cm from the top of piece no. 1 (Fig 5).

10. Now draw evenly spaced 2cm lines between the top of the no. 7 piece and the top of the no.1 piece – one will be on the centre line and the other two either side (Fig 2, left). Apply wood glue to each of the no. 8 pieces and stick them centred over each of the short vertical lines.

11. Apply wood glue to piece no. 10 and fix on the central vertical line drawn onto piece no. 1 earlier. The top of the attached no. 10 piece should touch the horizontal no. 7 piece and line up with piece no. 8 above that (Fig 2, right).

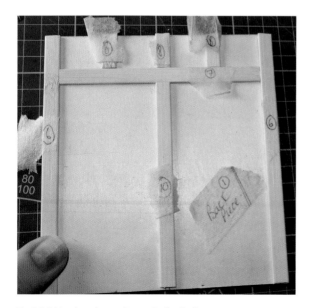

Fig 5 Sticking bamboo strips to the back piece.

12. Leave to dry for at least two hours. If necessary, put a heavy weight on top of any pieces not lying flat.

13. Once the glue has dried, rub down any edges that need tidying or realigning.

Bench Base

14. Apply a thin strip of wood glue along the short side outer edges of piece no 2. Attach the two base sides no. 4 flush with the bottom piece no. 2. Hold in place with paper tape or 3M medical tape at a 90-degree angle.

15. Apply a thin strip of wood glue to the outer vertical edges of the now attached no. 4 pieces, and the long edges of no. 2.

16. Fix in place the base front and back no. 3 pieces so that they are stuck to the no. 2 outer edges and the no. 4 vertical edges (the no. 3 pieces will be about 5mm taller than the side edges). Use the paper or medical tape to hold the pieces in place while they are drying. On the right of the image in Fig 6, a small wedge of wood has been used to fix a slightly too short side piece. This is a quick fix if there is no surplus wood available to cut a new piece. Simply place a small piece of wood to connect the two pieces (creating a join) and then coat the area with some wood glue.

Attaching the Back to the Base

17. Apply a stripe of wood glue along the bottom edge and bottom back of the back piece, as well as the inner base back (Fig 7).

18. Place the back piece inside the base piece and press against the glued area. Lay the back piece flat with the base up on its side (Fig 8). Place a 2mm-thick a piece of wood, bamboo or card underneath the back piece no. 1 to raise it slightly so that it dries level and in line with the base.

19. Fix the arm rests in place (again with the wood glue) to each lower outer edge of the back piece

Fig 6 Attaching the sides of the base.

Fig 7 Back and base connection: applying wood glue.

Fig 8 Back, base and side/arm connections in drying position.

no. 1 and the base piece no. 2 so that they sit inside the base sides. Fig 8 shows the positioning of arm rests.

20. Apply some extra glue to the inner area (wiping away any residue) and leave the piece to dry overnight.

21. Position and glue the three no. 9 pieces in line with the no. 6 and no. 10 pieces positioned earlier (Fig 9, overleaf).

22. At this point, check that you are happy with the look of the piece before proceeding. This is a good time to do more rubbing down, or soften some edges. Add aged affects if desired (as with the ceiling projects).

Staining and Sealing

23. The main frame of the piece is now completed and is ready to be stained with wood colour pens and scratch repair wood stain as for the Project 1 interior ceiling in Chapter 4. Any additional wood finial pieces can be added now for staining and colouring, or at some point in the future. Use the scratch repair pens to give the piece a solid base colour before staining (Fig 10, overleaf). Leave wood stain to dry overnight (check the manufacturer's instructions, as times may vary).

24. Seal with two-in-one sealant/varnish to help lock in the colour and to avoid contact stains with any fabrics.

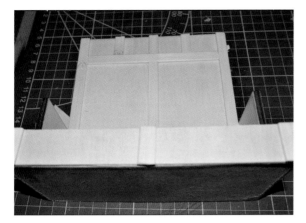

Fig 9 Fixing the no. 9 pieces in place.

Fig 10 Add any wood finials prior to colour, staining and varnishing.

Finishing Touches

Attach any desired finials or feet using either wood glue or nails and a small hammer. This piece used the following:

- 7mm × 8mm wood beads for feet (attached using small nails) and top edge decoration
- Silver jewellery-making strip (Etsy purchase) for the top edge
- Wood offcuts from an earlier project (shaped 4mm strips with triangle ends)
- Old necklace parts/links
- An old Tootal tie with heraldry images (charity shop purchase); ties often have small patterning that is perfect for 1:12 scale pieces, and contain a lot of material
- 2.5cm- to 3cm-thick craft sponge
- A4 piece of card

Fig 1 shows the Tudor bench with varying finials. One side shows the piece with the fabric inserts and one without (on the without piece, it would be possible to add an additional vertical bamboo strip to the centre of each side of the back; this was not done here to allow for fabric inserts in larger form). Any finials can be used – square, round, silver, wood and so on – but always keep the scale in mind. Choose small, patterned fabrics and leathers. Velvets, canvas and small tapestry fabrics work well for this type of piece.

Tooled leather was not actually used here but works beautifully for Tudor bench seats and chairs (*see* the four-poster bed project in Chapter 9 for the technique).

25. For each back piece insert, cut some thin card approximately 2mm smaller than the space to be filled. Fix the desired fabric to the cut cardboard pieces, making sure there is an overhang of around 10mm all the way round the pieces of card so that the fabric can be folded over and stuck to the back of the cardboard (Fig 11). Apply a thin layer of industrial superglue over the complete area where the insert is to go, and stick the fabric piece in place. Alternatively, fix the fabric with double-sided tape rather than sticking to card – sometimes this makes positioning a pattern or

Fig 11 Attaching fabric inserts. Cover pieces of card cut to size as shown.

attaching more delicate fabrics easier and helps to prevent creases.

26. For the cushioned seat, simply cut the sponge to size using a craft knife. If using a tie, such as the Tootal tie in this example, open up the tie (cutting the join seam carefully) and cut the fabric pieces to size for the cushion sponge piece (leaving enough for back piece inserts and, if possible, for a second piece of furniture).

27. Attach the chosen fabric to the sponge using double-sided fabric or carpet tape, in a similar way to the back piece inserts in step 25, except leaving a 5–7.5cm edge all the way round and cutting corner diagonals to make it easier to fold the fabric over the sponge edges (Fig 11). Glue the sponge into the inner space of the base using industrial-grade superglue.

At a later date, the coverings can be upgraded to hand-stitched fabric; for example, a hand-stitched (exposed outer stitching) ivory canvas-covered mattress or cushion can give a look of times past.

BUDGET BENCH

You do not need to add copious embellishments to the bench to create an authentic-looking miniature. Poorer households may have had a piece similar in style to this, but it would have had plain and practical fabrics and would be more likely to have had a plain back piece. This simple style suits most periods.

PROJECT 6: FOUR-POSTER BED

Fig 1 Four-poster bed: front and side views.

This chapter presents a project for a simple four-poster bed structure that you can adapt and change in the future, perhaps adding turned or hand-carved pieces or decorating with your own paintings or pyrography.

This simple construct can also be adapted by incorporating dovetail joins if this is a technique you have already mastered (or they can be added later). Fig 3 shows some common woodworking joints to experiment with, which strengthen pieces as well as enhancing their appearance. Some of the

projects in this book use simplified versions of some of these joins.

You would usually decorate each of the bed pieces – with tooled leather, carvings, pyrography, painting, wood stain and so on – prior to putting it together, but for clarity the instructions here show how to put the bed together in its untreated form, and deal with finishing details after it has been constructed.

All woods used are standard sizes (for 1:12 scale) and are readily available from crafting

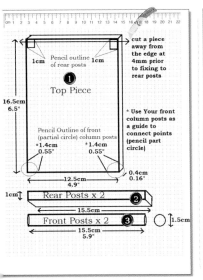
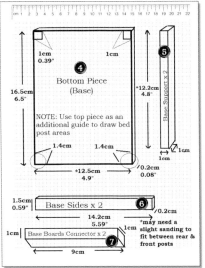
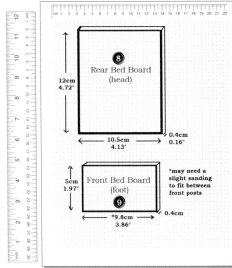

Fig 2 Four-poster bed plan.

stores or online (if you source pieces that are, say, 1mm thicker, simply adjust your measurements accordingly).

The woods used for the main frame of the bed in this project are all softer woods (balsa wood, lime, pine, basswood) and are thin enough to cut using simple hand-cutting tools. If using harder woods, you may need to use a table saw to cut simple lines and curves.

Once the piece is complete it will be coloured and stained (*see* Project 1 for staining instructions) and tooled leather additions and some finials will be added to give an antique finish. Some alternative methods for decorating your piece are also suggested.

This project is aimed at beginners, but there are also some additional tips and ideas for the more experienced miniature maker.

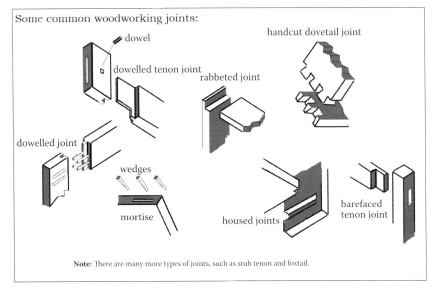

Fig 3 Common carpentry joints.

TOOLS AND MATERIALS

Note: finials and finishing materials are listed later in this chapter under Decoration

1. One pine wood panel sheet – approximately 250mm × 390mm × 4mm (saving offcuts for future projects), which is more than enough for pieces 1, 8 and 9
2. Two square pine wood sticks – approximately 300mm × 10mm for pieces 2, 5 and 7
3. Two oak wood rods – approximately 200mm × 15mm diameter for the no. 3 pieces
4. Two basswood sheets – approximately 200mm × 200mm × 2mm for pieces 4 and 6 (alternatively, measure the exact area required for pieces 4 and 6 and purchase a piece accordingly)
5. Cutting mat, placed on a solid surface, ideally a workbench or secure and solid wooden board used as a worktop
6. Metal ruler with finger guard
7. Craft knife, such as a Rolson or Stanley knife (a leather skiving knife may also be needed to thin any tooled leather)
8. Spare cutting blades
9. Small hacksaw or bow saw – with the correct blade for cutting metal
10. Tapes – Tesa paper tape and 3M medical tape
11. Sanding sponge or hand sander – coarse wet and dry for wood
12. Sanding files – semicircular and squared
13. Small hammer (optional) – useful for glued softer wood pieces (such as bedposts) if you need to add a nail to strengthen a join
14. Small nails (optional) – only use small craft nails (at least 14mm in length by approximately 1mm) and always test nails on an offcut to check it will not split
15. Strong wood glue and industrial-grade superglue
16. Mini wood planer (optional) – useful for any uneven edges on thinner woods that have been cut by hand
17. Safety mask, goggles and gloves (not shown)

Fig 4 Workbench with all required tools and materials.

STEP-BY-STEP GUIDE

1. Using the four-poster bed plan (Fig 2) as a guide, measure and mark each piece of wood ready for cutting, working on both sides of the flat for pieces that are over 2mm thick (pieces 1, 8 and 9).
2. Label each piece using some 3M-type tape and a pen (Fig 5).
3. The rounded front posts (no. 3 in Fig 5) should be measured around the diameter at several points and marked with small dots. These dots should be marked approximately 5mm apart all the way around each post to create an accurate guide for cutting. Then stick paper tape underneath the dots to create a line that will be scored and sawed in step 7 below.
4. Place pieces nos 1, 4, 6, 8 and 9 on the cutting mat.
5. Cut out these pieces using a craft knife and ruler, starting with a Stanley- or Rolson-type knife for the 4mm and 2mm pieces and switching to a finer craft knife when cutting the bedpost areas. Pieces nos 1, 8 and 9 will need to be cut from both sides of the wood. Leave the labels in place.
6. When hand cutting the areas where the round bedposts will sit into pieces nos 1 and 4, it is easiest to use push point (stab) cuts around the drawn areas – if you try to do a curve cut by hand, you will splinter the wood. Push the blade point down into dots on the curved dotted line, and use a gentle rocking motion to create a small cut until you reach the cutting mat; then the piece will simple drop out. Smooth the rough areas with a curved sanding file (using a side-to-side circular motion not an up-and-down motion).
7. Using a craft knife, gently score around the edge of the tape placed earlier around the cylindrical front posts (no. 3 in Fig 5). Ideally use a fixed clamp to hold the pieces in place. Use the small

Fig 5 Mark out wood pieces no.1 to no. 9 ready for scoring, cutting and sanding.

CUTTING WOOD PIECES FROM SHEETS

When cutting pieces of wood by hand using a craft knife and a ruler, you will find it easier if you mark your pieces from the outer edges of the wood so that you already have two straight edges before you begin. Pieces that are over 2mm thick will need several runs of the knife to achieve a full-depth cut and from both sides of the wood, so the template lines must be drawn on both sides. For pieces over 4mm thick you would need an electric saw, but all the wood used in this project is thinner than that.

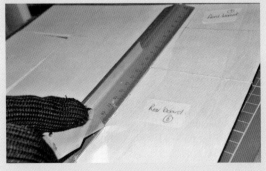

Fig 6 Cutting the 4mm thick pieces from both sides wearing cut-proof gloves.

hacksaw to saw the measured and scored length (follow the scored area to achieve a straight cut). This cut should be all the way through as this is cutting the posts to the correct length.

Use a sanding block or hand sander to smooth the cut area.

8. Mark and score the points where pieces 2 (rear posts), 5 (base supports) and 7 (bed board connectors) need to be cut (Fig 5). Ideally using a fixed clamp to hold the wood in place, cut the pieces to size using the small hacksaw at the measured and scored points. Use a sanding block to smooth the cut area.

9. Once all the pieces have been cut out, sand any rough edges, and if necessary, use the small plane for any straight edges that require levelling.

10. Before joining the bedposts to the base, make sure that the worktop is perfectly flat. Then lay the base onto a raised flat area 3cm off the worktop (for example, on a sanding sponge with the rear bed board on top). This will raise the base to the right height to glue the bedposts in place.

11. Apply a layer of industrial-grade superglue onto the cut-out corners of the base where the front and rear bedposts will sit. Be careful to glue only these areas (wipe away any excess with a cotton bud). Gently hold each bedpost in place against the glued area for about two minutes until it is secure.

12. Carefully apply some wood glue around the joins to fill any gaps and create a stronger connection (Fig 7). Be careful not to knock the posts whilst doing this as they could come loose (if they do, simply re-glue). Use a cotton bud to gently push the glue into the joins and wipe any excess with an alcohol wipe. The wood glue will usually take several hours to dry.

13. While the wood glue is drying, fix the base sides to the base. Apply a stripe of wood glue to the top inner edge (142mm long) and the side outer edges (2mm) of each base side and fix to the outer edges of both sides of the base (Fig 8). This is the perfect opportunity to straighten the bedposts where they join with the base sides,

Fig 7 Raise the base and glue on the front and rear bedposts.

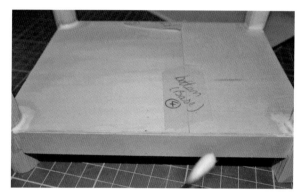

Fig 8 Attaching the base sides.

if required. Add another layer of wood glue to the joins using cotton buds, again wiping away any excess with an alcohol wipe. Leave the base, posts and sides to dry for at least three hours.

14. Apply wood glue to the 4mm inner side edges and bottom edges of both the headboard and footboard. Gently place the headboard between the rear posts with the bottom edge touching the outer edge of the base. Repeat with the footboard, placing it between the front posts (Fig 9). Carefully wipe away any glue residues.

15. To fix the top piece, first trim it by 4mm at the rear bedpost end with a craft knife (see Fig 2). Apply superglue to the inner edges of the bedpost cutouts on your top piece (front and rear). Gently slot the top piece between the front and rear bedposts to touch the top edges of

each post (Fig 10). Press the posts firmly against the top piece for a few minutes until a bond is created between the posts and the top piece. Once the piece is securely fixed, apply a layer of wood glue to the joins (filling any gaps and wiping away any residue). Allow to dry for approximately two to three hours.

16. Once the glue is dry, carefully turn over the bed on a flat surface to expose the underside of the base. Apply a layer of wood glue to one side of each of the base supports. Then apply a spot of wood glue to each of the inner bedposts against which the base supports will be placed. Fix the glued side of the two base supports to the base (one front and one rear) and push gently against the glued areas of the front and rear posts (Fig 11). Now apply a layer of wood glue to two adjacent sides of each of the two bed-board connectors. Fix one to the right-hand side of the base against the base side and one on the left. Allow to dry for at least one hour before turning over the piece.

17. Remove the tape labels from the bed pieces. Give the whole bed a gentle rub-down with a

hand sander or sanding sponge if necessary to create level joins where the bedposts join the top piece. Also rub down any areas where there is glue residue or staining.

This basic four-poster bed frame can now be adapted or decorated as desired. Fig 12 (overleaf) shows the exact same design only with square posts and some simple lathed front posts with additional trims. Larger-sized beds and half tester beds would also be straightforward adaptations.

Fig 10 Glue on the top piece.

Fig 9 Attaching the head and foot boards.

Fig 11 Adding the base supports and connectors.

To Lathe or not to Lathe?

Fig 12 Example of two designs from the same basic measurements but different levels of ornamentation.

Fig 13 Selection of items that can be used as finishing materials.

Decoration

As explained at the start of the chapter, normally each bed piece would be decorated prior to assembly. Techniques such as adding wood veneers and tooled leather are much easier to apply to flat pieces individually than they are to a constructed piece, and turning pillars on a lathe is obviously impossible once they are glued into place.

For this example project, however, we are going to add decorations post construction. Fig 13 shows a selection of items that can be used to decorate the completed four-poster bed. None of the finishing suggestions here requires carving, lathe or pyrography skills.

1. Use the wood repair pens to apply a solid colour over the areas of the bed and any wood

SUGGESTED MATERIALS

- Tableau Scratch Cover – Dark
- Wood repair pens – mixed colours
- Spare wooden Scrabble pieces
- Wood offcut from a damaged miniature – similar to many small wood clock finials or old picture frame tops
- Wooden mothballs and necklace beads
- Tooled leather cigar box – this one was found on eBay; tooled leather belts would also be perfect for bed sides and top edges
- Diffuser sticks in black
- Clear two-in-one varnish/sealant

TOOLS

- Small paintbrush
- Double-sided carpet tape
- Superglue
- Sandpaper or sanding sponge
- Craft knife
- Ruler

finials that will not be covered with tooled leather pieces. Start by mixing the colours unevenly and then cover with the chosen main colour (in this case black) to create solid coverage (Fig 14).

Fig 14 Apply uneven colour first (left) then a solid colour (right). Leave blank the areas the tooled leather will be attached to.

2. Fix in place any solid wood or metal finials. For this piece, the top wood offcut was added, along with some Scrabble squares (four for the bedpost bottoms and two for bedpost rear tops). Apply a coat of wood stain to all the areas coloured in step 1 (Tableau Scratch Cover used here); some seepage will occur naturally (Fig 15). Leave the bed to dry.

3. Strip the tooled leather piece by cutting out the patterns you wish to use with a craft knife and ruler, then carefully peel off the tooled leather (Fig 16). Cover the back of the pieces with strong double-sided carpet tape and then cut to size to fit the desired area. Peel back the double-sided sticky tape on the leather pieces and apply them to the chosen areas on the bed (Fig 17).

4. Tidy up any missed areas with wood pens. In this example, some black diffuser sticks were cut to size to tidy up any edges and to add a trim to some of the tooled leather pieces. Wooden beads were then glued on top.

5. Finally, add a thin coat of two-in-one wood varnish/sealant to the stained wood areas then put the bed to one side while it dries. Once the varnish is dry, you can add a mattress and bedding.

Fig 15 Attach the main finials and apply a coat of wood stain.

Fig 16 Preparing the tooled leather.

Fig 17 The finished bed showing areas of tooled leather decoration and added hand-stitched mattress.

CHAPTER 10

PROJECT 7: BABY CRIB

Fig 1 Baby crib in wood and repurposed metal tin.

This project for a baby crib combines some simple cut wood with a repurposed silver tin and basic finials. When reusing an existing object, rather than following strict measurements throughout, the materials should be cut to size by placing within or next to the piece itself for accuracy. Clearly not all tins will come with a pattern neatly in two halves like the one used here. Try to find one, however, that has an even pattern that will work well if cut in half – a central shield or crest pattern will not work well, for example.

That said, there is a to-scale baby crib plan supplied for this piece that you can simply adapt by replacing the tin object with a piece of similar size, whether it be in metal, wood or ceramic, or simply cut your own wood to size. The plan is a guide only and is not as extensive or precise as some of the other plans in this book as it will depend on the size of the object that you are repurposing; however, the measurements should roughly match the figures given here for a 1:12 scale representation of a baby crib.

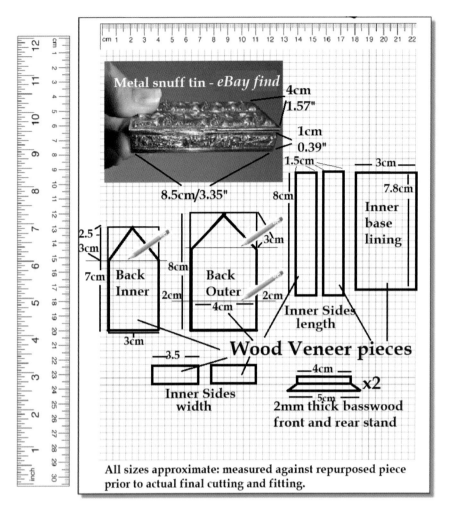

Fig 2 Plan for the baby crib.

Note: When using old pieces for repurposing, always check for hallmarks/provenance. Only use a piece if you are 100% sure it is suitable for repurposing.

Fig 3 Workbench with all required tools and materials.

TOOLS AND MATERIALS

1. One sheet wood veneer approximately 150mm × 200mm and 0.8mm–1mm thick
2. Bamboo skewer sticks
3. Selection of beads (wood and silver) for possible finials
4. Industrial-strength superglue
5. Strong wood glue
6. Two-in-one wood sealant and varnish
7. Wood stain
8. Wood offcuts from a prior project for possible finial use (optional)
9. Furniture touch-up pens in an assortment of colours (oak/cherry/mahogany/black) – to colour the wood veneer or any wood pieces used (optional)
10. Metallic marker pen in silver or gold – to add pattern or add a metallic edge to wood (optional)
11. Medium paintbrush
12. Cutting mat, placed on a solid surface, ideally a workbench or secure and solid wooden board used as a worktop
13. Craft knife
14. Spare cutting blades
15. Metal snippers (like Stanley FatMax)
16. Tapes – Tesa paper tape, 3M medical tape and double-sided paper and fabric tape (for crib insert)
17. Metal ruler with finger guard
18. Pencil
19. Solid and sturdy worktop/bench
20. Hand sanding sponges – wood wet and dry types
21. Safety mask (not shown)
22. Goggles (not shown)
23. Gloves (not shown)
24. Tin box for repurposing or wood pieces cut to size – approximately 85mm × 40mm × 10mm

STEP-BY-STEP GUIDE

1. Start by preparing the metal box, making sure to wear cut-proof gloves for these steps. To remove any hinged lid, gently bend the lid back and forth at the connected area until the hinged pieces naturally come loose. If this causes any misshaping, press the deformed area against a flat surface to push it back into place.
2. Cut the tin lid in half lengthways using tin cutters to create the sides of your crib hood (Fig 4). Trim about 2cm from the bottom of each piece so that each side hood piece is

Fig 4 Removing and cutting the tin lid.

approximately 6cm in length. (Alternatively cut two wood veneer strips to the same size and use these for the hood instead.)

3. Using Fig 2 as a guide, cut the back inner and back outer pieces from the sheet of wood veneer (no. 1 in Fig 3).

4. Cut the inner base lining to fit inside the tin, and fix in place with a thin layer of wood glue.

5. Cut two pieces of wood veneer to fit into each side of the tin – these are the inner sides length pieces in Fig 2. Each side piece should be approximately 5mm taller than the actual side of the tin. Do the same thing for the two inner sides width pieces. Add a thin layer of superglue to the tin inner edges and fix all the veneer inner sides into place (if necessary, use cotton buds to hold them in place).

6. Using the back inner wood veneer piece as a guide, mark the metal side pieces for the hood at the point where you will need to make a fold to follow the shape of the back inner. Wearing safety gloves, use a firm table edge or other box edge to fold the side pieces to the angle required to fit round the edge of the back inner wood piece (Fig 5). Any gaps (Fig 6) can be tidied later.

7. Trim the back inner wood piece sides if needed to fit into the back inner of your crib, leaving enough space on each side for the metal strips of the hood to fit it in place. Fix the metal sides into the tin inner with superglue, holding them in place for about two minutes until set (Fig 7 left). Place the trimmings from the hood side pieces (*see* step 2) inside the inside edges to tidy up the spot where the tin sides are fixed (Fig 7 right).

8. Fix the back outer piece behind the back inner (whose sides are now fixed) with wood glue. Hold in place with 3M or paper tape. Once the glue has dried, trim the outer hood to the desired finish. In Fig 7 (right), the back outer piece is slightly taller than the back inner piece in order to add strength to the whole of the hood and hide any gaps between wood inner hood and tin sides.

9. Cut the bamboo skewer sticks to size to cover any untidy edges and remaining gaps (Fig 8).

10. Cut two bamboo skewer sticks (keeping one end of each stick pointy) to the desired length to fix to the rear sides of the crib hood with a thin layer of superglue (pointy end upwards). Cut two slightly shorter bamboo skewer sticks (again keeping one end of each stick pointy) and similarly fix to the front sides of the crib hood (again pointy end upwards).

11. Once the sticks are fixed into place, put a small dot of superglue on each pointy end and then

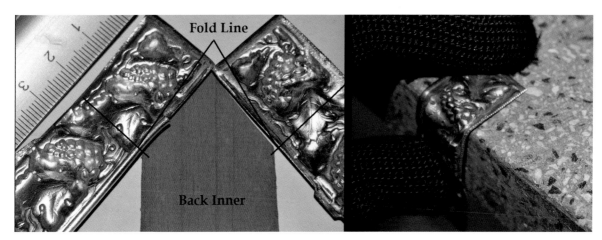

Fig 5 Marking and bending the side hood pieces.

Fig 6 Using the back inner veneer as a guide for the fold angle.

place a small bead on top, threading the point of each skewer into the hole of the bead (Fig 9).

12. Add any desired finial to the top of the hood to fill the gap between the two tin sides. Here a simple rectangle was cut from the 1mm wood veneer used earlier and glued to the top to seal the gap, and then a slightly smaller rectangular piece, from the same wood veneer, was added underneath to conceal the tin side joins. Finally, another smaller fencepost-shaped piece – clearly visible in Fig 11 – was added on top of the rectangle.

13. Cut the two front and rear stands (as shown in Fig 2) from a 2mm-thick piece of basswood. Each piece is a made from two strips that are approximately 5mm high and then glued together to create a 10mm-high piece. Once the glue has dried, they can be fixed into place on the front and rear outer edges with superglue (Fig 10). The stands can be adapted if desired, for example by using curved pieces to make a rocking cradle.

14. Rub down any rough edges and larger wood areas with a sanding block or sponge.

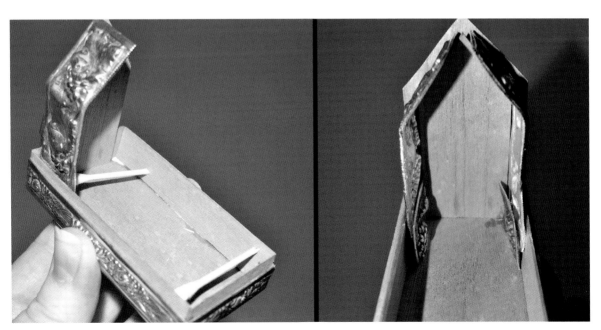

Fig 7 The hood with the back inner and outer pieces fitted.

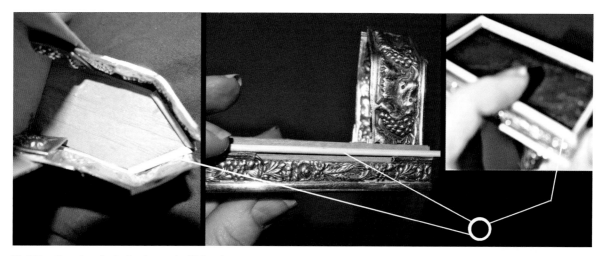

Fig 8 Line the edges (including bottom) with bamboo.

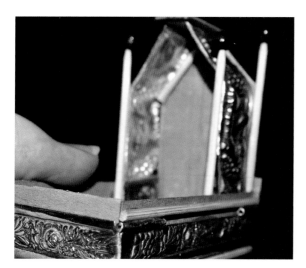

Fig 9 Fixing bamboo finials with balls to the crib hood.

15. To colour the finished crib, use the furniture repair pens to give a dark wood finish to all the wood/ bamboo areas (the black works well over any areas where you may still have glue residue). Then cover the coloured areas with wood stain – in this example, Tableau Scratch Cover in Dark (Fig 11). Wipe away any wood stain that comes into contact with the metal using a cotton bud or some lint-free cloth.

Fig 10 Front and rear stands fixed (shown here stained).

Fig 11 Colouring and staining.

Fig 12 Adding a fabric insert for bedding.

16. Once dried, give the wood areas a light coat of sealant and varnish.

17. Once the varnish is completely dry, add a fabric insert or mattress to the crib if desired. A simple way to do this is by cutting a thin piece of card into the inner area shape (less about 2mm around the edge). Now stick a layer of double-sided tape to both sides of the card and cover it with fabric (with an excess of about 5mm, which can be folded over and stuck to the back of the card). It can be fixed permanently in place or simply be laid in the crib as a removable piece. To give a slightly cushioned feel, fix slightly smaller fabric rectangles to the cut card before covering with the main outer fabric. In this piece, a darker velvet insert was used (Fig 12) to reduce the risk of any colour transfer occurring between the wood and fabric (which can sometimes happen even after sealing).

CHAPTER 11

PROJECT 8: BOOKCASE WITH HANDMADE BOOKS

This chapter presents a project for a bookcase along with some great tips for getting started on making your own 1:12 scale books. Bookcases are usually quite straightforward in their main construct (not including edgings/finials), as they usually comprise mainly varying sizes of rectangles.

All the shelves make the project a little fiddly, however, but bear in mind that the time the wood glue takes to set gives you plenty of opportunity to position pieces accurately and apply fixing tape to hold them in place. There will undoubtedly be some glue residues left that can simply be sanded away once the glued areas are completely dry.

As for previous projects, this one shows the piece being constructed in bare wood to show the stages more clearly. In practice, however, it is highly advisable to colour and stain the wood pieces before assembly as it will be very hard to access all the small internal spaces once the bookcase is put together. Using the wood stain method (pens then stain), colour or stain the back piece inner, the inner sides and the three middle shelf pieces prior to assembly. Alternatively, use a paint such as Decorlack Glossy Black acrylic, which is easily applied with a small brush and gives great coverage, even in small spaces. Add some of this type of paint to areas of stained wood to give a matched and timeworn appearance.

Fig 1 Antique stained bookcase in a black finish with books and scrolls, arranged three different ways.

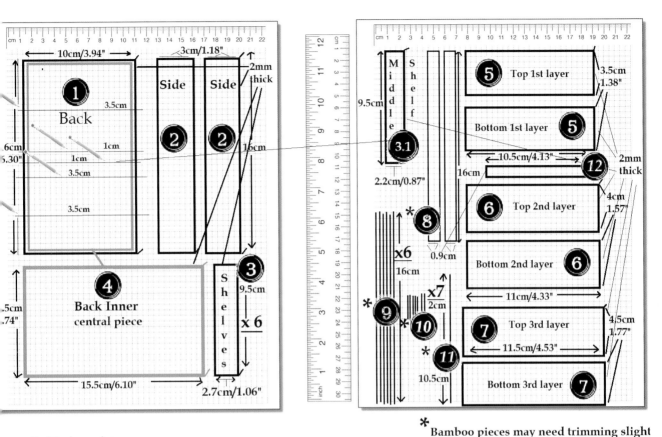

Fig 2 Bookcase plan.

* **Bamboo pieces may need trimming slight**

Fig 3 Farrow & Ball paint colour card with some sample tins.

The piece also works well in its bare wood form as a lighter piece, and you may opt simply to varnish or paint in lighter colours. Farrow & Ball is a British manufacturer of beautiful paints based mainly on historic archives that are perfect for this type of historical 1:12 scale miniature. They have a large colour palette to choose from in different finishes, reflecting many periods in history, and a sample tin goes a long way when painting 1:12 scale furniture.

TOOLS AND MATERIALS

1. Three basswood sheets – approximately 200mm × 300mm × 2mm
2. Wood veneer sheets (optional) – fixed to bare wood with wood glue, weighted face down on a flat surface to dry, then trimmed and rubbed down
3. Strong wood glue and industrial-strength superglue – Crocodile wood glue used here along with Everbuild superglue (the two types shown are liquid and gel versions of same glue)
4. Wood stain – Tableau Scratch Cover in Dark used here
5. Cardboard sheet, 2mm thick (optional) – use for no. 4 inner piece as a wood alternative if you do not have enough wood; it takes wood stain well
6. Three bamboo crafting strips, each 400mm × 9mm × 3mm
7. Furniture repair pens
8. Cutting mat, placed on a solid surface, ideally a workbench or secure and solid wooden board used as a worktop
9. Workbench or solid and secure worktop
10. Two-in-one wood sealant and varnish – Contura used here (optional)
11. Selection of finials in wood, leather and metal – for example old beads, necklace parts and miniature offcuts (optional)
12. Decorlack acrylic paint in Glossy Black (optional)
13. Seven bamboo skewer sticks
14. Craft knife and spare blades
15. Sanding sponge or hand sander – coarse and fine wet and dry for wood
16. Tapes – Tesa paper tape, 3M medical tape and double-sided paper and fabric tape (for the books)
17. Metal ruler with finger guard
18. Pencil
19. Some basic book- and scroll-making items (mainly for fixed, non-opening books) – printable book covers/inners, printable maps/scrolls, Scrabble pieces, tooled leather offcuts
20. Crafting tweezers (not shown) – come in flat or curved variations and are usually longer than regular medical tweezers
21. Safety mask, goggles and gloves (not shown)

Fig 4 Workbench with all required tools and materials.

STEP-BY-STEP GUIDE

1. Using Fig 2 as a guide, measure and mark each piece of wood ready for cutting.
2. Label each piece using some 3M or paper tape and a pen.
3. Place the pieces on the cutting mat and, wearing cut-proof safety gloves, cut out each piece using a craft knife and ruler. Leave the labels in place.
4. Sand smooth any rough edges using a sanding block or sponge.
5. Coat the back of the no. 4 back inner piece with a thin layer of wood glue and place it on top of the no. 1 back piece, leaving an even border around the edge. Use weights to hold the piece flat and in place while drying (Fig 6).
6. Once the glue has dried, draw pencil lines onto the glued-together back piece for lining up the shelves later, as shown in Fig 2.
7. Attach the side pieces with wood glue applied to the border left around the back inner piece no. 4 when it was stuck to piece no. 1. Hold the pieces in place with paper tape and support in position with blocks or boxes.
8. Attach one no. 3 shelf piece at the top of the back piece between the side pieces, and another at the bottom, effectively creating an open box (Fig 7).
9. Fixing the remaining four no. 3 internal shelf pieces in place (leaving the middle slot empty for piece no. 3.1) by adding a thin layer of glue to the outer three edges that will slot into the frame of the bookcase. Line the shelves up with the lines drawn in step 6. Once the shelves are lined up and sit straight, wipe away any glue residue and leave the shelves to dry in place. (Use paper and/or 3M tape for additional support if necessary, but keep in mind that this will need to be removed very carefully – crafting tweezers are useful for this purpose.)
10. Once the shelves are dried into place, fix the last internal shelf – no. 3.1 – in the same way to line up with the middle line (Fig 8).
11. Take the seven no. 10 bamboo sticks that will divide the middle shelf into slots for scrolls, and trim each one down individually prior to putting

Fig 5 Mark out the pieces, label, cut and sand.

Fig 6 Fixing the inner piece to the back before weighting down to dry.

Fig 7 Fixing the side, top and bottom pieces.

Fig 8 Fitting the internal shelves.

into place across the front of shelf 3.1. Add a spot of wood glue to the top and bottom tip of each piece and then a spot of glue on the edge of shelf 3.1 at the place where it will rest (make sure the sticks are spread evenly across the width of the bookcase). Fitting the sticks is quite fiddly – it may be easiest to pop them into place with a pair of craft tweezers. Leave to dry.

12. Lay the bookcase flat on its back and glue in place (with wood glue) the top and bottom no. 5 pieces squarely over the top and bottom of the bookcase. Repeat this process for the no. 6 pieces, sticking them over the no. 5s, and then again for the no. 7s.

13. Trim the no. 8 pieces if necessary to fit lengthways down each side of the front of the bookcase. Cut the bamboo strips (no. 9) to the same length as the no. 8 pieces and glue three onto each no. 8 piece side by side to give a ridged effect. Weigh down if needed to keep in place while drying (Fig 9 left).

14. Trim down the no. 11 bamboo stick and attach it to the top edge of the newly fixed no. 9 pieces so that it hides any uneven ends and creates a tidy edging at the top of the bookcase.

15. Trim down the no. 12 piece and use it to edge the bottom part of the bookcase and cover the lower part of the no. 9 pieces (Fig 9 right).

Fig 9 Attaching the outer edges and trims.

16. Once all the pieces are fixed in place, gently rub down the whole bookcase ready for any staining, painting or varnish applications.

17. Wooden details should be added now so they receive the same colour or staining treatment as the rest of the wardrobe. In this example, four wooden beads were added for feet and two ball finials on the top at each front corner. More ornate carved finials, such as corbels, trims and columns could also be added, or a top piece such as a broken bonnet, which is quite a simple shape to cut and fix into place.

18. Colour and stain the piece in the same way as for the four-poster bed and Tudor bench (Projects 5 and 6).

19. To achieve the finish shown in this example, then paint the internal area of the bookcase (including shelves) with Decorlack Glossy Black paint using a very small paintbrush. This paint is great for darkening corners and disguising any tricky glue stains. (Remember, this would normally be done before construction along with the staining.)

20. Once the stain and paint has dried (allow 48 hours to be on the safe side), coat the whole piece in two-in-one wood seal and varnish and leave in a safe place to dry. This will be the final

Fig 10 Colouring and staining.

step whether or not the staining and painting was carried out before construction or not.

Display Books

Overleaf is a quick method for making non-opening fixed books for display purposes only. Figure 11 does include some opening books, which can be found online by searching for items such as 'miniature printable book'. Simply print off these pages and cut and fix them into your own miniature book spine/covers (as used for your non-opening books).

Fig 11 Materials for making miniature books.

Below is a list of tools and materials.

- Old or craft Scrabble tiles – for books glued into place in shorter shelves (where the book inner will not be visible)
- Thin card
- Craft card for non-opening book inner – 380g/m²
- Ivory paint
- 1:12 scale book printables, scrolls, maps or drawings (searchable online); alternatively scale down images of your own choice to create your own collection
- Printer
- Printable canvas – Simplicity PhotoFabric Cotton Poplin used here; alternatively just use paper
- Thin tooled leather
- Thin leather
- Parchment paper (for scrolls)
- Thin red string, plaited cotton or tassel – for scroll ties and book page separators
- PVA glue
- Mod Podge water-based sealer, glue and finish, clear – Matte Antique version used here
- Glue applicator or toothpick
- Craft knife or scissors

The following instructions can be used to make the display books.

1. Source 1:12 scale book printables, scrolls, maps or artwork. Ready edited and scaled examples can be found for free online. Alternatively, scan and scale down your own titles. Use software such as Paintshop Pro/Paintshop Pro Ultimate to help edit the scanned images.
2. Print the pages off onto printable canvas or paper. If using canvas, it is worth doing a test print first on paper first, as the printable canvas can be quite expensive in comparison, at about £20 for five A4 sheets. The result is very authentic, however; this type of printable fabric is often used by miniaturists for tapestry and carpets.
3. Stick the printed book printables and/or tooled leather to some thin card with PVA glue (Fig 12). Weigh down flat and wait for glue to dry.
4. Cut out the book printables or tooled leather. Go round the outer edge of your cut books with a thin (do not press too hard) line of marker pen; try to match book colour or go slightly darker (Fig 13). This will not only conceal any differentiation between card and book printable but will also create a slight seepage into the printable fabric, giving it a natural aged look. When using printable canvas or cotton poplin, you will notice some fraying threads; this is nothing to worry about as these will be trimmed later before adding a coat of Mod Podge to seal.

Fig 12 Glue the printed 1:12 scale books to a thin piece of card.

Fig 13 Cut out the book covers and mark the edges.

5. Measure the space from spine to outer edges of the book printable and cut the 380g/m² card to size (Fig 14). Depending on the thickness of the spine, it may be necessary to cut several pieces of card to stick together to fill the spine space to create a page effect. Now stick the board pieces together and press down firmly. Here nine pieces were used for the larger-sized book and seven for the medium. Once dried, the edges can be evened up with a hand sander or sanding sponge.

6. Paint the three edges of the 380g/m² card that will be exposed with a chosen colour; ivory is good for older books, brown for an antique look and gold for religious and more expensive volumes.

7. Using a ruler or desk edge, fold the book printables over on each side of the spine (Fig 15).

8. Add a thin layer of PVA glue on one side of the book inner 380g/m² card and the spine and insert into the book cover, then press into place. Add a page turner string, or piece of plaited cotton or tassel if desired to the inner edge of spine on the side not yet glued and dangle over outer side of spine. Add layer of glue to side of the board not glued and then press down the last piece of the book printable. Weigh down and leave to dry.

Fig 14 Cutting card for the book inners.

Fig 15 Folding the spine. Here, the edge of workbench was used.

Fig 16 Mod Podge is applied to prevent fraying.

9. Trim any loose threads and untidy edges (go round the edge with pen again if needed). Add a thin coat of Mod Podge to the book printable, making sure to cover the edges, as this will help to prevent any loose threads or shedding (Fig 16). The Mod Podge will seal in the colour and give a leather-like aged look. A matt version was used for this example, but for a more pristine or new-book look, gloss might be preferable.

10. Place the completed books in the bookcase or miniature scene.

The Scrabble pieces are perfect for small non-opening books that will be fixed somewhere that will not expose what would be the page area.

Some larger books were also added to this 1:12 scale bookcase and work well to represent perhaps an atlas or a set of encyclopaedia, which wealthier households would have had. A Victorian accountant, for example, would often have large ledger books (usually leather bound) that would take up almost a third of a desktop. Most books, however, would

Fig 17 One full-size old book with various 1:12 scale books.

Fig 18 Making scrolls.

have been much smaller. Figure 17 shows a full-size antique book beside a selection of different-sized 1:12 scale books (opening and non-opening) all made using the same printable cover style and all suitable for the 1:12 scale setting (as patterning remains within scale); the smaller Scrabble-size book would be the normal size for perhaps a novel or poetry book.

AUTHENTIC-LOOKING BOOKS

Always keep in mind the setting and purpose of your books and scrolls and pick an appropriate size and design. Whether it be a large book or small, remember the text and images should still be in 1:12 scale as well as the cover patterning.

Scrolls

Scrolls can be quickly made using the simple steps below.

1. Print off and cut out the chosen 1:12 scale printables (maps, art, text and so on) onto parchment paper or printable canvas, or simple copier paper. You can also opt to do double-sided prints.
2. Stick tape to parts of the prints. Tear it away then rub down lightly to create an aged effect (Fig 19).
3. Lightly moisten a finger with some water (do not use too much) and then dip it into cinnamon powder. Rub the cinnamon over parts of the printables to create staining (Fig 20).

4. Curl and/or fold the corners of the scroll. Roll the scroll up around a small glue stick or paintbrush. Add a little spot of glue to the underside of the rolled outer edge to hold it in place, then slide it off the glue stick (or paintbrush).

5. Tie or fix the scroll as desired – for example with string, velvet, tassels or wax. When using hot wax, always follow the manufacturer's safety instructions.

6. If the scrolls are to be fixed in place – for example in the centre section of the bookcase – it is quicker to make longer scrolls, then cut them in half and slot both into place.

There are other more advanced aging methods that require more extensive instruction and safety recommendations, such as scorching, but the methods mentioned here are a good starting point.

Fig 19 Tearing and rubbing the printed images to create a worn look.

Fig 20 Use a spice such as cinnamon to create a stained and aged look.

CHAPTER 12

PROJECT 9: FANTASY PIECE – THE FAIRY KING'S THRONE

Fig 1 The Fairy King's Throne in 1:12 scale.

The project in this chapter is intended to be an inspiration piece for a fantasy setting. The Fairy King doll was made for me by the wonderful MidDreamers fairy artist Lisa Morrow, whose work is available on Etsy.

Previous projects in this book have looked at scratch-built pieces and ones using both handmade and repurposed materials (such as the fireplace in Project 2). Now this project will demonstrate how thinking outside the box and viewing common objects from a different perspective can help you create beautiful fantasy pieces.

The main item you will need in order to make a piece similar to this is an old metal gravy boat.

Using pieces like this not only enables you to craft imaginative pieces but also, and very importantly, recycles and repurposes items that were often mass produced and are now largely thrown away.

The actual gravy boat used in this project was heavily damaged at the base and the silver plating was very badly chipped away, but thankfully the seller had the good sense to add it to his table at a car boot sale and sell it as a scrap piece (often these sorts of pieces simply get put out with the rubbish). I originally envisioned it as a hot-air-balloon carriage (and already drilled holes around the edges for the chain ropes) and it could also have worked well as a small boat bed or a Roman chariot – just to give an idea of the versatility of pieces like this.

At the end of this project, there is a list of just some of the items to look out for that are ideal for repurposing into 1:12 scale pieces, along with suggestions for what they could be turned into. You will often find suitable pieces by foraging through markets, charity shops, websites like Etsy or eBay and car boot sales.

CHECK THE ITEM'S VALUE

When using old materials – like the sauce boat in this project – always exercise due diligence and check the piece's provenance and value before repurposing to ensure that you are not about to ruin a possibly valuable antique or historically significant artefact. Items such as highly carved picture frames, silver-plated gravy boats and pressed tin cigarette boxes would have been made in relatively large numbers (especially since the nineteenth century) and can still be widely found today, but nevertheless it is always wise to have a quick check for markings, hallmarks, signatures, signature features and patterning and so on.

Fig 2 The metal gravy boat used for the throne – before and after.

TOOLS AND MATERIALS

1. Gravy or sauce boat
2. Support piece – this one was sourced from another car boot sale and was possibly a box or bowl stand. Alternatives could be some wooden balls or scrolled jewellery box corner feet, or for this theme, even a small piece of driftwood or wood from the forest floor
3. Back-up support piece (optional) – it's always good to have a second choice. This was an old brass piece found on eBay; the idea would have been to simply turn the chariot standing area around and then use it as the back support piece to hold the gravy boat upright (with a few modifications)
4. Fabric offcuts – used here was a mustard velvet offcut from an old velvet top approximately 20cm × 20cm for the main piece and 10cm × 10cm for the cushioned area (folded in half to 10cm × 5cm)
5. Choice of finials (optional) – to finish the piece or tidy up sharp or blunt ends. Included here was a small globe, some wooden beads and (hidden at the bottom) a few glass and metal beads
6. Scrap tissue paper
7. Colour primer for metal – needed as a key for the enamel topcoat as it will not paint/grip well to the metal without it. The Army Painter Colour Primer in Leather Brown was used here (choose a colour closest to your chosen enamel topcoat)
8. Industrial-grade superglue – used here was Everbuild Superglue (CYN50) Industrial Utilisation and Rite Lok (MC100) for metal joins
9. Enamel paint – Revell 32180 gloss brown was used here (a 14ml tin is sufficient – a little goes a long way with this paint)
10. Sanding sponge – coarse wet and dry for wood/metal/plastic; a metal file may be required where the base is removed
11. Tin shears or metal cutter – Stanley FatMax tin shears used here
12. Small hacksaw or bow saw (optional) – with the correct blade for cutting metal
13. Scissors (optional)
14. Tapes – paper tape, 3M medical tape and double-sided fabric tape (about 15mm wide). 3M medical tape and Tesa Eco paper tape work well for masking (covering areas you do not wish to get colour on) as both stick well and are

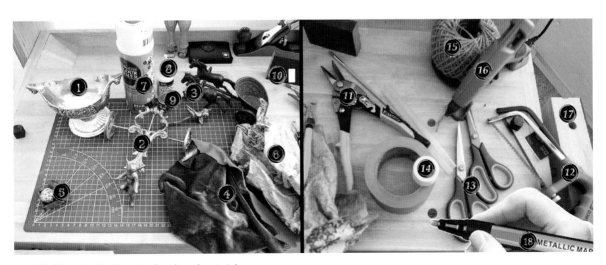

Fig 3 Workbench with all required tools and materials.

easy to tear; medical tape is especially good for non-flat surfaces

15. Something to rest the upside-down gravy boat on – used here was an old parcel string stand, but a small tin of food would do as well

16. Hot-glue gun and glue sticks (optional) – may not be needed as the industrial superglue is often strong enough to hold smaller, lighter metal pieces together (and was not used in this project). Very heavy pieces may even require use of a soldering iron

17. Workbench with vice/grip (optional) – very useful for rubbing down the gravy boat and cutting off the gravy-boat base. Stand-alone vices can also be screwed or clamped to a workbench

18. Metallic marker pen – used here was a Funnasting silver metallic marker

19. Safety mask, goggles and gloves (not shown)

A cutting mat is optional, ideally one that is self-healing; any grids, shapes and metrics on it will be useful for future projects.

STEP-BY-STEP GUIDE

Preparing the Gravy Boat

1. Using the small hacksaw or tin cutters, and wearing cut-proof gloves, remove the base of the gravy boat (Fig 4). For this piece, the hacksaw was best as it was easier to saw at the join point than to cut. Any rough edges will need to rubbed down with a metal file and/or sanding sponge.

2. Wearing a safety mask, sand down the smooth surface area of the underside of the gravy boat to create a key for the undercoat. It's not necessary to remove the whole surface area but simply create a slightly rough texture. Focus on sanding the circular area where the base joined the main

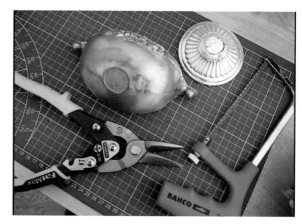
Fig 4 Remove the stand from the gravy boat.

Fig 5 Rub down the metal to create a key for undercoat to cling to.

body, as this is likely to be slightly raised; try to get this as smooth as possible (Fig 5). A vice is useful to hold the piece in place; otherwise, hold it in one hand and sand with the other – it will achieve the same result but may take a little longer.

3. Either fold or stitch the 10cm × 10cm piece of fabric offcut to create a small cushion of approximately 10cm × 5cm. Place this inside the gravy boat to create a slightly padded area at one end, and fix it in place with the industrial superglue (Fig 6). This does not have to be

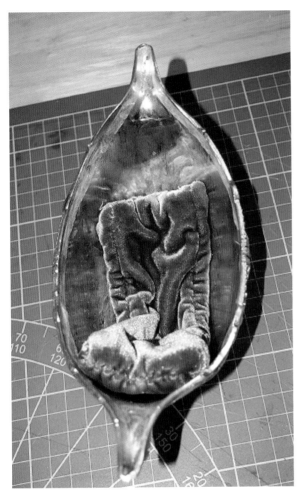

Fig 6 Add a small cushioned area.

Fig 7 Prepare the top inner edge to hold the larger fabric offcut.

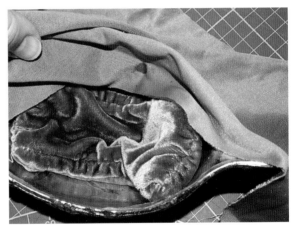

Fig 8 Attaching the larger fabric offcut.

perfect, as this area will be covered later with the main piece of fabric.

4. Tear or cut a length of fabric tape to line the top inner edge of both sides of the gravy boat. Remove the outer cover of the fabric tape and coat the exposed strip with a thin layer of industrial-strength superglue, wiping away any excess glue that runs down into the inner section to avoid staining fabric that will cover this area (Fig 7).

5. Press the larger, 20cm × 20cm piece of fabric offcut around the top inner edge against the double-sided fabric tape. Press about 2cm of the fabric onto the tape, with the fabric underside facing you as you go round the edge (Fig 8). Once you are almost all the way round, tuck any excess fabric into the gravy boat and then press the final piece from the outside, exposing the top side of fabric. Allow the glue to set for about 30 minutes.

6. Secure the fabric inside the gravy boat with 3M tape (Fig 9) to keep it out of the way of the undercoat/primer and enamel applications.

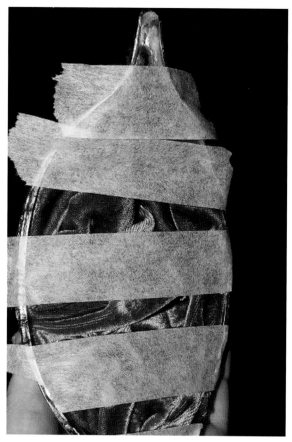

Fig 9 Secure the fabric before painting.

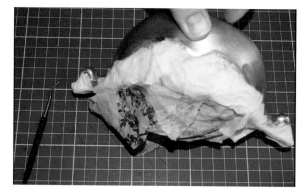

Fig 10 Mask the areas where you do not want paint to go.

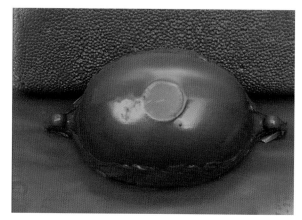

Fig 11 Primer spray application.

7. Mask the areas on the underside that you do not wish to paint using scrap tissue paper stuck down with 3M or paper tape (Fig 10); for this piece, the flower-patterned areas were masked. A small applicator tool, as shown in the image, or a cotton bud can be useful to push tape around edges.

8. Place the gravy boat upside down in a well-ventilated area on a flat surface, covered with old newspaper, and spray a thin coat of colour primer for metal over the entire exposed area (Fig 11). Follow the instructions on the colour primer product and wear the appropriate protective mask and goggles. Once the primer is dry, move the gravy boat – trying not to touch the painted area – back to the workbench and rest it on top of a secure object that will support it without it wobbling (Fig 12).

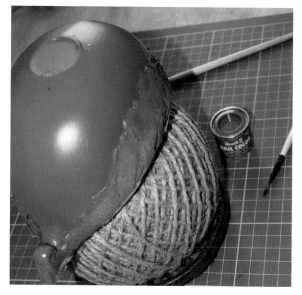

Fig 12 Rest the gravy boat on a support piece ready for enamelling.

9. The gravy boat is now ready for its enamel coat. Again, read the manufacturer's instructions in full and put on goggles and an appropriate face mask before beginning. Use a small, fine model-painting paintbrush (Revell have their own range of these) to apply a thin coat to the exposed surface of the gravy boat, brushing out any areas where the paint has been applied too thickly as you go. Once the first coat is dry, a second coat can be added if necessary. Leave it to dry for at least 24 hours (Fig 13).

10. Once the enamel coat has dried, leave the gravy boat in position on its secure support and gently remove the 3M or paper tape and tissue paper (avoid touching the painted area). There will nearly always be some seepage of paint that gets through to the covered areas, and this is where the silver marker pen comes in. A magnification lamp will help to identify more easily the areas that need to be tidied up (Fig 14). Use the marker to cover any areas that the enamel has seeped onto, while being

Fig 14 Tidying up any accidentally painted areas with a silver marker pen.

careful not to go onto the area that should be enamelled. The silver marker used here is by Funnasting and is great for this purpose because it does not work like a paint marker (the kind that need shaking and often have to be pressed to release paint, which often results in too much release in one go). If using the latter type, shake and press the pen onto a separate piece of card first before working on the desired area.

Preparing the Base

11. Now it's time to work on the base piece. The base used in this project was a broken stand of some kind bought at a car boot sale. Any old metal piece should firstly be given a clean with soap and water, then dried thoroughly with a lint-free cloth.

12. If required, give the base a light rub-down with the sanding sponge. Be careful when doing this on metal pieces not to lose any definition on patterned areas.

Fig 13 Apply a single coat of enamel paint to the exposed surface.

13. To create a support piece to hold the gravy boat in the desired position, the base was cut at the points shown in Fig 15 (A) and then glued into an upright angled position as shown in (B). You may need to do this or something similar depending on the piece you decide to use for the base. Always wear protective goggles and the appropriate safety mask when working with strong adhesives.

14. The industrial-grade superglue was found to be sufficient to hold the newly upright part in place, but it would have required soldering in place had it been heavier. The piece was supported with a sanding sponge while it dried in the upright position as show in Fig 16 (point A). Any glue or solder residue must be wiped away.

15. Allow the part to set for at least twelve hours. If you are using heavier metal pieces, you may opt to use a hot-glue gun to join the areas (hold in place whilst it sets) or even a soldering iron (always strictly following the manufacturer's guidelines for use and safety).

16. Apply industrial superglue to the base parts where the gravy boat will rest (Fig 16, points B); lightly place the gravy boat in position first to identify where these points are. Carefully wipe away any glue drips.

17. Before fixing the gravy boat onto the base, make sure that any heavy support pieces required to keep the gravy boat in position whilst the glue sets are ready; in this case a heavy wood plane was used for this purpose (Fig 17). Hold the gravy boat at each tip and gently lower it into position, making sure that the cushioned area is facing the front. Touch the front part to the glued area of the base first and then slowly lower the rear part into position. Hold it in place with one hand and move the support items into position to hold the piece still whilst the glue sets. Leave to dry for a minimum of twelve hours.

Finials

This piece had a broken piece (cherub) that was simply positioned as a finial at the top point of the gravy boat. Furthermore, a broken rear piece from the stand was used as a join between the stand and the gravy boat (where it touches the back enamelled area). Using parts from one component of a piece on

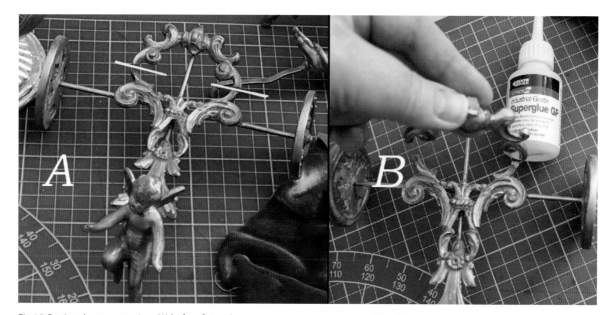

Fig 15 Cutting the support piece (A) before fixing the cut section into an upright position (B).

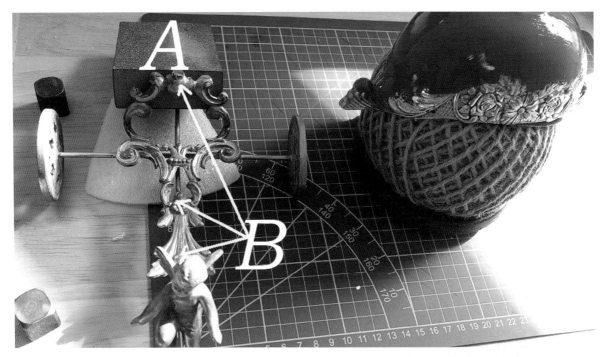

Fig 16 Hold the support piece in place while the glue is drying with a sanding sponge or similar block (A), then apply glue to the points where the gravy boat will rest (B).

the other is a great way of partnering them to look like one original piece.

Small wooden beads were taken from an old necklace and added to the top and back of the gravy boat – a handy way to conceal joins (Fig 18).

Two glass and metal beads were also added to the back, where there was an exposed metal rod tip and where the cherub metal support strip joined the enamelled rear of the gravy boat, also shown in Fig 18.

At this point, it is good to run a final check over the piece to see if there are any areas that need tidying up (with silver marker, for example). Otherwise, the throne is completed!

Repurposing

Below is a list of just a few old items that are perfect for repurposing and some possible uses:

- Old, tooled leather belts – look for small patterns, which are perfect for trims and edgings and easy to cut with crafting knife
- Old, tooled leather cigar or jewellery boxes – as above but also perfect for covering larger areas such as fireplaces, bed heads and footboards
- Ties – often handmade or embroidered with small patterns
- Old petit point cosmetic and purse bags – often have small patterns, which are perfect for covering for seating and creating tapestry-look upholstery
- Clock finials – search for broken clock cases or finials online or at car boot sales. Often they will have beautiful column work and finials (for example cherubs, lion faces, Atlas holding a globe, angels, flowers – to name but a few)

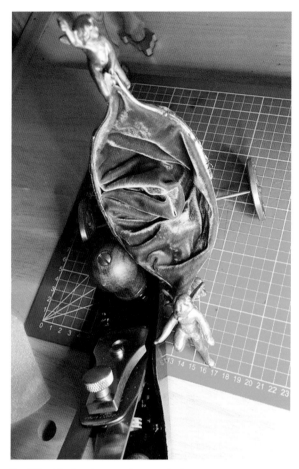

Fig 17 Positioning the gravy boat on the base.

Fig 18 The yellow lines indicate where finials are added.

- Old jewellery boxes – such as the popular 1950s Tallent brand boxes that were produced in high numbers and often resemble medieval or Tudor panelling
- Brass or other metal pressed cigarette tins – now often unhinged and with signs of age or damage, but they can be found with beautiful patterns and images and, because they were designed to fit in a pocket, the pattern size is often perfect for 1:12 scale pieces such as fireplace back plates
- Letter/business card cases – often in metal. One example of a piece made using a business card carrier is the Georgian swing boat shown here. A 1920s card case was used for the frame and then a scratch-built walnut wood boat was

attached with some created swing mechanism pieces to enable the piece to move back and forth. Silver trim was added to the boat to match it to the repurposed card holder.
- Embroidered bookmarks – often found in museum gift shops or charity shops and sometimes have small designs perfect for upholstering and curtains
- Scrap wood/offcuts – including old clock parts. Search online for old clock parts, clock finials, wood blanks, clock columns, reclaimed wood and so on, and you may find pieces perfect for repurposing and sometimes wood blanks that can be used for carving or on the lathe. Mixed scrap wood bundles often include apple, walnut, cherry and pear woods

Repurposed 1920 business card carrier combined with scratch-built boat to make a swing boat.

- Old jewellery – old wooden bead necklaces and decorated enamel pieces can be found in charity shops, at markets or boot sales and online. There are many ways old jewellery can be incorporated into miniature making: beads, for example make good finials and furniture feet, and small wood and silver bangles and bracelets can be used to create a bed canopy. Look out for pieces that have small patterning, carving or imagery
- Old tiles – some tiles have small decorative patterns perfect for interior wall decors (again be mindful of the scale). Old tiles are used as part of the room box project in Chapter 14
- Silver or other metal gravy boats and small trinket boxes – look for tiny details such as trinket boxes with pressed metal images or small paintings on them. Also look for pieces that are footed (often have small ball feet or ball and claw feet). For gravy boats, go for either plain or small-patterned pieces and always choose ones that have a separate base to the main body that can be later removed easily using tools (rather than one moulded piece)

CLEVER SEARCHING

Think outside the box when searching for items (online or at markets/boot sales). Typing 'putti cherub' into a search engine, for example, is likely to throw up more expensive options than 'old metal angel' or 'old wood cherub', even if you may have to sift through more results to find what you're looking for. Similarly, when looking for clock cases or finials, avoid using famous makers' names as their pieces will inevitably be more expensive, and search for 'bits and pieces' rather than 'finials'. Make the most of the fact that you don't need the item to be in working order – look for 'broken clock case' or 'old damaged clock' and you may easily find a bargain.

You may love a good antiques fair and may have been fortunate enough to find some great pieces at great prices, but the fact that it is called an 'antiques' market does indicate that the sellers there are more likely to have researched their wares and priced them accordingly. On the plus side, such markets will have such an abundance of wares that you are very likely to find something to pique your interest or give you ideas of what to look out for from alternative avenues.

Charity shops and car boot sales (do not be afraid to rummage through the baskets often set on the ground) can be the source of great bargains but you must be prepared to make many visits to many boot sales and be aware that a lot of the time you will come away with nothing. Check online for local car boot sales and their opening times.

CHAPTER 13

PROJECT 10: ARCHITECT'S DESK

Fig 1 The finished desk with architect figure.

The antique style architect's desk in this project would suit settings from the sixteenth century right through to modern times – desks of this type are still made and are in use today. (The doll show in Fig 1 is a 1:12 scale male ball-jointed doll made for me by Zjakazumi, whose work can be found on Etsy.)

The finished desk could also be for a painter, artist, engineer or craftsman; simply add some accessories to reflect your chosen theme, such as a half-finished painting with some paintbrushes or engineering images along with measurement tools.

This project will introduce handmade 1:12 scale miniatures that have moving parts, in this case the tiltable desktop.

TOOLS AND MATERIALS

1. Wood lathe (optional) – for the side pieces on the desktop area; alternatively, use plain rod dowels (*see* no. 4) topped with wooden beads
2. One pine wood panel sheet – approximately 250mm × 390mm × 4mm
3. Three bamboo craft strips – each 400mm × 9mm × 3mm long
4. Mixed wood pieces for the sides of the desk top piece and bottom dowel; homemade lathed pieces used here but it is also possible to purchase rod dowels with grooves, which would work well for the side pieces, with a wooden bead finial for example. You will need a 3–4mm-diameter wooden rod dowel to slot between the two side A pieces (*see* Fig 3) and support the bottom desk piece, and at least two 20cm-long dowels to allow for the slot piece and the side pieces comfortably
5. Two laser-cut wagon wheels or metal rings (only one is actually required, but it's best to have two to allow for errors, as these are quite delicate) – at least 45mm in diameter but not thicker than 3.25mm. Laser-cut wagon wheels can be bought online and at craft stores. Brass or other metal rings of the same size can be found in old clock/watch parts (for example gears) or bought online. If using a metal ring, you will need to use a small saw with a suitable blade for cutting metal
6. Strong wood glue and industrial-strength superglue – Crocodile wood glue used here, along with Everbuild industrial superglue
7. Wood stain – Tableau Scratch Cover in Dark used here
8. Decorlack acrylic paint in Glossy Black
9. Three small paintbrushes
10. Furniture repair pens
11. Farrow & Ball sample paint for desk top, middle and bottom sections – Pale Powder used here
12. Mixed finials and trims
13. Cutting mat, placed on a solid surface, ideally some sort of workbench or secure and solid worktop
14. Workbench or secure worktop

Fig 2 Workbench with all required tools and materials.

15. Craft knife and spare blades
16. Coping saw for crafting – for cutting curved pieces by hand; alternatively cut the side pieces to a straight-sided shape with a craft knife, or repurpose any suitable wood pieces
17. Sanding sponge or hand sander – coarse and fine wet and dry for wood
18. Needle file – for sanding and refining the cut wagon wheel
19. Small drill tool – shown here is a Dremel multi-type drill for crafting and a non-electric hand drill by The Army Painter; the drill bit will need to be the correct size for the dowel hole pieces (3–4mm)
20. Metal ruler with finger guard
21. Sharp pencil and silver marker – Faber-Castell pencil and Funnasting metallic marker used here
22. Sharp scissors (optional) – only needed to cut prints as decorative additions to the piece
23. Tapes – Tesa paper tape and 3M medical tape (not shown)
24. Drill gauge – for correct drill bit measurement (not shown)
25. Safety mask, goggles and gloves (not shown)

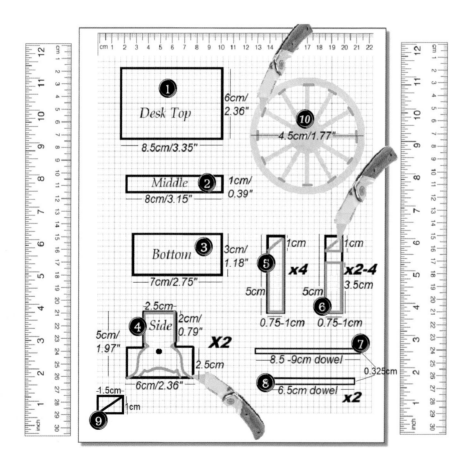

Fig 3 Architect's desk plan.

STEP-BY-STEP GUIDE

Preparing the Pieces

1. Place the wood panel sheet onto the cutting mat. Using Fig 3 as a guide, measure and draw out the pieces to be cut out on the wood panel. Label each piece of wood using 3M or paper tape ready for cutting (Fig 4). The side A pieces can be adapted to your own design but keep the bottom length at 6cm for balance and top length at 2.5cm. Fig 4 shows three different example shapes.

2. Use the correct saw or knife for cutting out the chosen design for piece no. 4. For straight lines, cut with a craft knife from both sides of the board or use the small hacksaw; when cutting curves, choose the coping saw and/or crafting blades, depending on skill level.

3. If using a metal ring instead of the wood wagon-wheel piece, cut the ring in half using a small saw with a metal-cutting blade. With a wood wagon wheel, the spindles need to be removed, as shown in Fig 4 (no. 10). Use a needle file to sand flat any wheel spoke joins on the cut half wheel pieces.

4. Sand smooth any rough edges on all the pieces.

5. Using a manual or electric drill, bore a small hole through each no. 4 piece roughly in the middle (approximately 30mm from widest point and 23mm from the bottom) as shown in Fig 3. The hole should be the right size to snugly fit dowel rod piece no. 8; here the drill gauge was adjusted for a 0.325cm diameter. Use a round needle file to make the hole slightly larger if needed.

4. Stain and paint any pieces that may be more difficult to do once the piece is put together. This applies mainly to the top, middle and bottom sections, and the long dowel piece. Test any paint or stain on an offcut first. Fig 5 shows the cut no. 4 pieces and joining dowel coloured and stained, and the top, middle and bottom pieces coloured with the chosen Farrow & Ball paint.

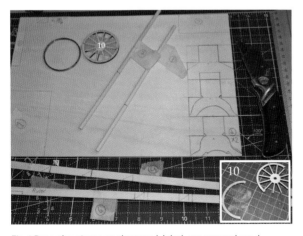

Fig 4 Draw the pieces on the wood, label, cut out and sand.

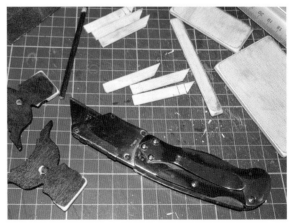

Fig 5 Test the stain and paint on offcuts first.

5. Once the paint is dry, some grey lines and texture can be added with a pencil. Gently rub the area with a fine sanding sponge in the same direction as the lines to blend and achieve a worn look. Use a coarse hand sander or sanding sponge to soften the edges and corners of the top, middle and bottom pieces. To achieve a newer look, miss out the pencil lines and just rub down the edges and corners less, or miss this stage out all together.

6. Glue together the no. 5 and 6 pieces from Fig 3 (one set for each side of the desk), as shown in Fig 6. Before firmly gluing everything in place, check that the half ring (no. 10 in Fig 4) fits through the gap in piece no. 6 (between the two no. 5 pieces). If the half ring is too thick to slot though the gap, then either thin the wood wheel (by sanding with a wood-shaving tool) or simply add an additional no. 6 piece (so two no. 6 pieces will be glued together in between a no. 5 piece on each side). Once both sets of pieces are glued together with the correct-sized gap, rub down the edges so that they are even and the sides match each other.

Assembly

7. Start by gluing (with industrial superglue) each of the combined no. 5 and 6 piece sets centrally to the top of the no. 4 pieces, as shown in Fig 7 (hold in place until set).

8. Now glue the no. 2 middle piece in place (Fig 7). Apply superglue to the area that the no. 2 piece will touch on each of the no. 4 pieces and on the bottom edge of the combined no. 5 and 6 pieces. Hold the piece carefully in position while the glue sets, with the no. 4 pieces lying flat on the cutting mat.

9. Apply superglue to each of the holes in the no. 4 pieces. Carefully slot dowel piece no. 7 into one of the no. 4 pieces so that is flush with the outside, then carefully slot the other end into the other no. 4 piece. There will be some flexibility to move the base frame while you are fitting the dowel in place until glue sets. Trim or rub down any excess on overlaps where necessary.

10. Apply a thin layer of superglue to the upper side of the no. 7 connecting dowel rod between the two no. 4 pieces about 5mm from each edge. Position the no. 3 bottom piece centrally onto

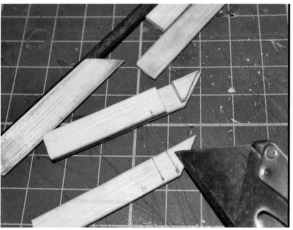

Fig 6 Gluing together the nos 5 and 6 pieces.

Fig 7 Gluing the base frame pieces.

11. Now carefully thread both of half ring pieces through the slotted hole area of the combined nos 5 and 6 pieces. Add a spot of industrial-strength superglue to the end tips of each half circle and stick to the back side of the top no. 1 piece as shown in Fig 8. Hold in position until fixed. Leave to dry for a little longer before testing the rotation of the desktop.

12. Figure 10 shows the desk with fitted carved and lathed sidebars, but plain dowel rod pieces (no. 8 on the plan) can be used instead, adorned, if desired, with wood bead finials. The purpose of the side bars is for the user to hold to rotate the desktop into the desired position. Simply apply a thin layer of superglue along the outer sides of the no. 1 desktop piece and hold the bars in place until fixed.

13. The paper rest shown in Fig 10 was cut by hand. Use a 25mm cut piece of dowel or alternatively add a paper rest using a finial such as the curved metal drawer handle shown amongst the finial pieces (no. 12) in Fig 2.

the glued area and hold in position until fixed in place (Fig 8). Now position the two triangular no. 9 pieces between the no. 4 pieces and the top of piece no. 3, as shown in Fig 9, by adding glue to each outer edge and fixing into place. These give additional support to the bottom shelf piece now glued to the dowel.

Fig 8 Gluing the top, bottom and half ring.

Fig 9 Fixing support triangles.

Fig 10 Side bars and paper rest.

Fig 11 Staining, colouring and sealing.

Staining, Colouring and Sealing

14. Colour and stain any remaining areas as desired. Here the Decorlack was used to finish the no. 4 pieces and the half circles (Fig 11). The side bars were coloured using the scratch repair pens and a little wood stain. The top, middle and bottom were painted prior to assembly in step 4, along with the joining dowel rod.

15. If using the Decorlack or something similar, wait for it to dry and then add some evenly spaced silver dots (using a fine-tipped silver paint marker) to the outer edge of the half circle rings to give the appearance of metal studs.

16. Once the piece is completely dry, add a layer of two-in-one sealant/varnish to the dark-painted and wood-stained areas (not to the top, middle and bottom sections if a Farrow & Ball-type lighter paint finish was used).

Finishing Touches

17. To make the ruler, use a piece of leftover bamboo strip from piece no. 6. Cut a piece approximately 7cm long with a craft knife, and then cut it in half vertically (so the finished dimensions will be 70cm × 0.5cm). Cut a small piece of the 4mm-thick wood used for piece no. 1 to about 1.5cm wide by 0.75cm high. Score a hole in the centre of the cut 4mm piece and screw the bamboo piece to it using a mini eyelet screw, as shown in the finials in Fig 2 (no. 12). For further decoration, a small circular piece, such as a miniature doorknob surround or a small metal washer, can be fitted before attaching the eyelet screw. Add the ruler markings by hand with a sharp pencil.

18. The small circular drawing tool is made using the same method as the ruler but with smaller pieces and a pointed short end instead of a flat end. Experiment a little with pressure points here as the wood can split; however, with a bit of practice, and by scoring holes before screwing, it should be easily achievable. If necessary, add some glue to split areas and conceal with a bit of rubbing down and some strategic staining and painting. Figure 1 shows the ruler and circular tool in place.

19. The architectural image used in Fig 1 was sourced online and printed onto standard copier paper to fit the desktop; some additions were made by hand to show measurements and notes. Of course, any kind of image could be used here to suit your theme, printed onto paper or canvas.

The next chapter will cover how to include this piece in a themed setting.

CHAPTER 14

PROJECT 11: ARCHITECT'S ROOM BOX

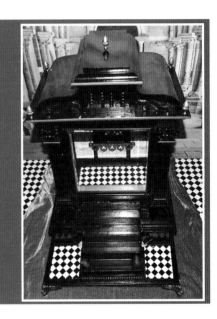

Fig 1 Antique-style room box.

This chapter presents an inspiration project for an antique-style architect's room box, the aim being to inspire you to make your own piece after sourcing your own materials and then applying the methods you choose to take from this project. Techniques covered in earlier chapters will also be revisited and combined. The architect's room box in Fig 1 was made from a repurposed clock case.

Alternatively, you can replicate or create your own version of this room box by cutting out wood pieces to similar measurements and adding your own design elements

THE IMPORTANCE OF SCALE

Always keep the 1:12 scale in mind when searching for pieces. The clock case example shown in this chapter is at the smaller end in width and depth, though the height is perfect. You can also seek out larger items for repurposing in order to create settings such as a dining hall that will hold multiple 1:12 scale pieces of furniture.

TOOLS AND MATERIALS

1. Old clock case (Fig 2) or cabinet for repurposing – minimum internal clear space required for a small scene such as shown in Fig 1 is 20cm wide × 11.5cm deep × 22cm tall; increase measurements accordingly for larger scenes
2. Mixed wood sheets and wood blanks (if required): 4mm/2mm sheets and 1mm veneer sheets as well as wood blanks for steps (either one larger blank to be cut into step shape using a bench saw or smaller blanks connected to create steps); some projects of this type may not require additional steps
3. Bamboo crafting strips (optional) – each 400mm × 9mm × 3mm – for any border trims
4. Black diffuser sticks (optional) – for any edgings; these are often also available in other colours such as green and red
5. Wooden rod dowels (optional) – 3–4mm in diameter; another good choice for edgings

Fig 2 An old clock case with non-working clock.

Fig 3 Workbench with all required tools and materials.

6. 1:12 scale wood skirting (optional) – usual size for skirting needs to be in range of 15mm × 3mm × length required; cut your own or buy from many dolls' house building suppliers (*see* appendices for details)

7. Wood stain (optional) – Tableau Scratch Cover in Dark used here

8. Decorlack acrylic paint in Glossy Black

9. Adhesives – wood glue, industrial-strength superglue and Mod Podge Antique Matte; the last will only be needed if you are adding paper or canvas mural/wall prints

10. Two-in-one wood sealant and varnish – Contura used here

11. Liquitex Professional acrylic marker – available in many shades; Iridescent Antique Gold used here

12. Wood repair pens

13. Metal ruler with finger guard

14. Coaster tiles (optional) – for decorating the ceiling area; the ones used in this project are 'Catania' by Patrizia Bellini (*see* appendices)

15. Mixed cabinet latches and hinges (if required)

16. Alternative ceiling piece (optional) – can be made following the instructions in Project 1, adjusted to the required size (*see* Chapter 4)

17. Windows (optional) – make your own or add a laser-cut window such as the one shown here, by Viorica (*see* appendices for supplier details), or search for kits online

18. Cut glass for windows (optional) – glass pieces (often cut to size) can be bought online

19. Sharp pair of scissors

20. Craft knife and spare blades – a Rolson was used here

21. Self-adhesive felt – shown here in graphite and brown (graphite used for this project); available from most crafting sites and stores

22. Sanding sponge or hand sander – coarse and fine wet and dry for wood

23. Tapes – Tesa paper tape, 3M medical tape and strong double-sided sticky tape

24. Printable canvas fabric – Simplicity canvas used here

25. Flooring (optional) – tiny black and white ceramic tiles used here are by Tiny Ceramics (*see* appendices); another option would be a stone floor or wooden floorboards

26. Screwdriver with changeable heads – Bosch rechargeable screwdriver shown here; manual screwdrivers can be used instead

27. Mixed finials (optional) – examples shown here include wooden mothballs, wood hand-cut beads, mixed handles (to add to top of piece to make it a carry piece), brass and silver clock finials

28. Corner feet (optional) – available in varied sizes and often found on jewellery boxes and small cabinets; for this piece the feet used were 42mm × 30mm. If you prefer to have the piece sit flat, add felt gliders to protect the surfaces the piece may sit upon and/or decorative corners

29. Pencil

30. Tile cutter(s) (if required) – only needed if using tiles

31. Small drill (optional) – with pilot-hole drill piece and then a larger drill piece, for creating support holes for final ball pieces on the bottom step if desired (not shown)

32. Cutting mat on a solid worktop or workbench

33. Safety goggles and gloves (not shown)

A small mallet or hammer (if required) will be needed if dismantling the piece to be repurposed rather than using as it is.

STEP-BY-STEP GUIDE FOR THE EXAMPLE PIECE

1. This clock case had non-working mechanical clock parts within in it as well as the clock face, all of which needed to be removed; mostly these can be removed simply using a flat-head and/or Phillips screwdriver (Fig 4). Store any parts for later (either for repair or for repurposing).

Fig 4 Removing any inner parts from the clock case.

Many old clock cases will not have the actual mechanical pieces present.

2. With the clock inners removed (Fig 5), it is possible to work out the basic design for the piece.

For this clock case, for example, there were two main options: simply remove the back door and move the window-shaped area now exposed (which had held the clock face in place) from the front of the piece to the back; or carefully dismantle the wood pieces and put the clock case back together (like a jigsaw) to create the exact positioning required for the imagined piece.

The easiest option would have been the first one, but for the purposes of this book, it was more useful for the reader to be shown how to repurpose a clock case using all of its parts (except, in this case, the rear door) by dismantling and putting it back together in full. Presenting the project in this way will give you a basic understanding on how to make such a piece even if parts of the clock or cabinet case you have sourced are very damaged or even missing (simply replace missing pieces

Fig 5 Front and back view of the clock case with inners removed.

Fig 6 Dismantled clock case.

Fig 7 Adding steps.

with cut-to-size alternatives). The clock case was dismantled quite easily by using a small mallet tapped upwards from the inside to remove firstly the top piece and then the sides and so on. The square window-shaped section was left attached to the two sides. Fig 6 shows the dismantled clock case.

The Base and Steps

3. Because the main door for this piece (framed glass) did not sit directly on the base, a step area was incorporated in the design. This meant that an additional base support area needed to be added. This was done by measuring the base of the clock area and adding the depth of the steps to the front, then simply cutting two pieces of 4mm-thick wood sheets to a square size for the original clock base area with added steps to be fixed upon later. The two cut pieces of 4mm wood were then glued together with wood glue and weighted down while they dried. Once dry, the now 8mm base piece was put to one side for later (when the clock case would be reassembled into the desired design).

   If your item for repurposing has a main door that sits flush with its base, an additional base

will not be needed; you could add one if desired, however, to fit embellishments such as columns, statues or tiles and so on.

4. A set of steps were made to fit on the front of the clock case by first measuring the distance from the actual base of clock to the opening door space (to give the height required for the steps, which should then be reduced by approximately 3mm), and deciding how wide the steps should be. A space was then cut into the front of the base for the completed steps to slot into so that they would sit flush with the main frame of the clock case; the cut lines on the base in Fig 7 indicate the section that needed to be removed.

5. The space where the steps were to go was measured to determine the size the steps needed to be. There are many methods for making steps. These ones were cut from one solid block of wood 114mm deep × 89mm tall × 127mm wide using a table saw (each step being just under 25mm).

   The steps were then coloured with wood stain and varnished, before being painted over later with black Decorlack. It was mentioned earlier that wood is very forgiving, and this is a case in point – if you change your mind on colour, just wait for the application to fully dry and then sand down the piece completely to create a new key for your final choice of colour.

You do not have to cut your steps from one solid block of wood; instead you can opt to make them from wood blanks (basswood, for example), cut to desired width and then glued together and sanded down. Keep in mind the scale (about 25mm-square blanks are fine for 1:12 scale). Figure 8 shows just two of the many ways that you can make steps and stairs out of wood blanks. The first simply stacks the blanks on top of each other. For the second, each blank is cut in half with a table saw along the cut line shown, then glued to a cut-to-size flat 2–4mm board as shown in the bottom left of the image.

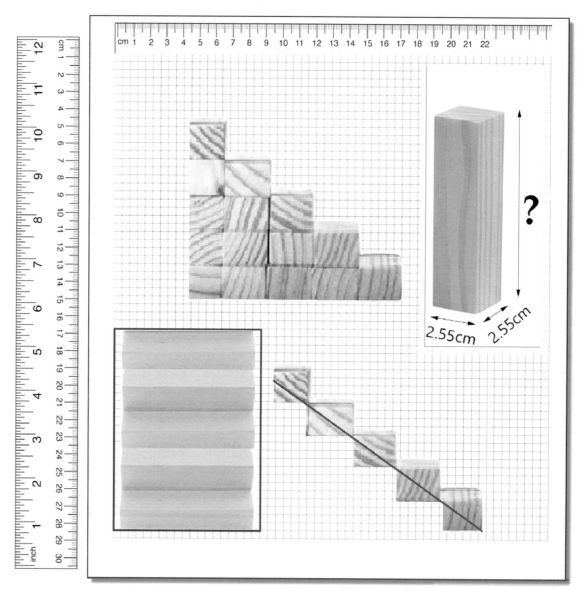

Fig 8 Two ways to make steps.

The edges of the board would then be trimmed and the sides rubbed down so all steps are level with each other.

6. Using a generous amount of wood glue, the main frame of the room box and the newly cut steps were glued into place onto the 8mm base piece created in step 3 (Fig 9). Prior to gluing the steps in place, two small pilot holes were drilled into the side of each bottom step followed by a larger hole (to support the two wooden ball pieces that would be added as finials later).

7. The steps were then edged with some cut-to-size bamboo strips to conceal any uneven edges or gaps.

8. The glued pieces were then left for at least twelve hours to dry in place and then the base piece was trimmed to be flush with the back and sides of the clock case and in line with the front of the steps.

Internal Walls and Floor

9. Next the wall decoration was chosen for the internal space. Architectural prints were sourced and printed onto the printable canvas to the desired sizes, leaving some white space around edges (Fig 10). Any theme could be chosen here – for example mathematical equations for a mathematician or the solar system for an astronomer. Alternatively, you could add 1:12 scale wallpaper (available from many sellers online) or in larger spaces simply install miniature bookcases, wall panels and so on.

10. Strong double-sided sticky tape was applied to the back of the images and then the printed canvas was trimmed once again to fit each of the walls to which it was to be applied. The window area image was cut in half and the window area cut and folded with a craft knife once it was in place (Fig 11).

11. Smaller, matching images were added to the space above and below the window to fill the gaps.

Fig 9 Main frame assembly.

Fig 10 Pictures to decorate the walls in the desired theme.

Fig 11 Fixing the canvas in place.

Fig 12 Edging the canvas.

12. A thin coat of Mod Podge was then applied to the now fixed-in-place canvas, to prevent the edges from fraying.

13. Once the canvas walls were dry, they were each edged with some black diffuser sticks and bamboo strips to frame the canvas sides and the window area (keeping in mind the space needed to install the window piece later). A plain skirting was then added around the bottom edges of each wall (Fig 12).

14. Black and white ceramic tiles were chosen to decorate the inner floor and the two spaces beside the outer steps. To tile a space of this type, cut a piece of card or 2mm basswood to the exact size of the inner floor space. Then draw a line between each pair of opposite corners to make an X to determine the centre point. Using the industrial-strength superglue, fix the first piece to the middle point (either diamond or square facing depending on the desired look; for this piece, a diamond pattern was chosen). Then fix the rest of the tiles into place around it until the card is full.

15. Once the tiled pieces were dry, the edges were trimmed using a pair of tile cutters. Do not worry if you have some cracked tiles in the trimmed area,

as they can be concealed by adding a bamboo border (as was done in this case; *see* step 16).

16. Both the inner floor piece and the outer edge pieces were glued into their relative positions and edged with bamboo strips, which were then painted black using Decorlack Glossy Black (these do not need to be sanded to create a key for the Decorlack as they are untreated and will therefore absorb the paint). A coat of the same paint was also added to the front, front edges and the steps (Fig 13).

Fig 13 The woodwork was painted black.

Windows

17. The working window used for this piece came in kit form; two kits were purchased so that one could be fitted to the inside of the room box and one to the outside. Before fitting, the window pieces were stained with dark wood stain and then sealed with a sealant (to prevent any contact staining spoiling the canvas prints). The frame section of the window kit was painted using the same Decorlack Glossy Black as used for the bamboo edging earlier (Fig 14).

18. Inner and outer window pieces were fitted into the window space with wood glue and left to dry. Once they were dry, some finials were added (patterned metal ledge trim, wood beading, window handle and a window pull for the inside of the exterior window).

19. The gap between the inner and outer windows was then painted black (no sanding was required as the gap was paint- and varnish-free). No glass was added to this window piece, but this could easily be done if desired. Fig 15 shows the fitted window.

Fig 15 The fitted window.

Ceiling

20. The top part on this particular clock case had a hollow inner space that was perfect for placing tiles into; however, if your piece does not have

Fig 14 Windows stained and painted prior to fitting.

this, simply add tiles or a ceiling piece to the flat area instead (just avoid adding decoration to the places where the top will be fixed to the main frame). Patterned coaster tiles (with a pattern suitable for 1:12 scale) were glued with industrial-strength superglue into the inner top space. Painted bamboo strips and black diffuser sticks were cut to size and added to the joins and edges to give an impression of beams (Fig 16).

There are many alternative ceiling styles you could opt for, including the wood ceiling piece from Project 1. Measure the space to be filled and fit the wood bamboo strips – with a smaller gap in between the vertical pieces for a smaller room box (such as this one).

21. Any internal edges were then sanded down and tided up with a coat of black Decorlack paint. (Sanding down any previously painted

Fig 16 Decorating the ceiling with tiles.

or varnished areas will create a key for the new paint to adhere to.)

22. The top part with completed ceiling was then glued to the main frame of the clock case using strong wood glue.

23. Once the ceiling was completely fixed in place, the door could be fitted, and was attached to the right side of the main frame using the original hinges. Which side of the room box the door is hinged to is a matter of personal taste.

Finishings and Finials

The following finishings and finials were added to the piece in the order stated:

24. Bamboo strips were painted black and used to trim the outer edges of the base piece.

25. Graphite self-adhesive felt was cut to size to cover the underside of the base piece and then the brass corner feet screwed in place (Fig 17).

26. A second coat of Decorlack added to already painted areas. The top piece was then sanded down along with other larger areas of the clock case exterior that were to be painted with Decorlack (this is needed to create a surface the paint will adhere to), including the front columns and the back.

27. Some small beading was added to the central square area on the top piece and then painted black.

28. The Liquitex gold paint pen was used to add a gold edge to the two rims of the top piece as well as on the front columns.

Fig 17 Attaching feet to the felt underside.

29. Two small scroll pieces were added to each of the rear side base areas where the steps join.

30. Industrial-strength superglue was poured carefully into the pre-drilled holes on each side of the bottom step made in step 6. A wood mothball was fixed to each of the holes and then stained with scratch repair wood stain.

31. The door latch was positioned and screwed on (Fig 18).

32. Five repurposed clock acorn finials (from another clock) were added to the four corners of the clock piece and to the centre top.

33. A final coat of Decorlack was applied to any areas that needed it.

34. Once the clock was complete, the architect's desk from Chapter 14 was added along with a few additional pieces, including the architect himself (Fig 19).

LIGHTING

If you wish to add lighting to your room box, there are two ways to do so. One approach is to drill wire holes and lay down lines before putting the piece together. Alternatively, you can opt for 1:12 scale battery-powered pieces, such as melted candles, that could be fixed to a small piece of furniture with the battery compartment hidden inside the piece. Drill a small hole, thread the cable through and into the provided plug piece; it will be powered by a single battery connecter for lighting (often referred to as a '9V battery connector with wire fits 12V lamps for dollhouse'). The Miniature Scene of York is a terrific source for such items.

Fig 18 Attaching a door latch.

Fig 19 The architect's room box with resident architect.

CHAPTER 15

PROJECT 12: KITCHEN DRESSER

Fig 1 A magnificent eighteenth-century kitchen dresser with broken bonnet top.

This project is an introduction to combining plans and designs. It will also introduce two electrical tools that will make things a little easier for projects of this type: one is for cutting small wood strips when a large amount of the same piece is required, and the other is for cutting thicker sections of wood. Both are good entry-level electric tools for novice miniaturists and a practical addition to any miniature maker's tool kit. However, neither is essential to complete this project.

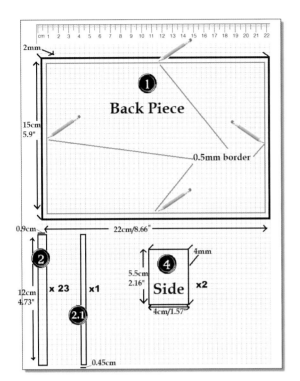

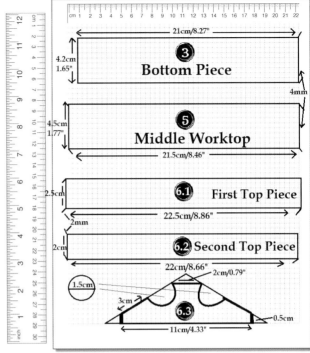

*Bamboo strips: approx 0.9cm wide

Pieces 3, 4 and 5 can also be cut from 2mm sheets (simply double up), *see* **steps.**

Fig 2 Kitchen dresser plan part 1.

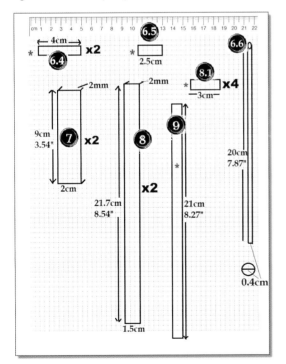

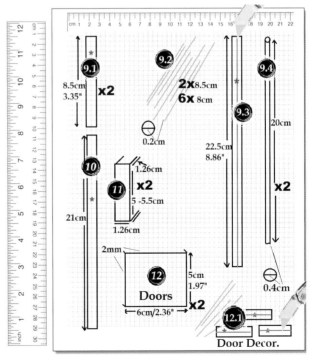

*Bamboo strips: approx 0.9cm wide

Fig 3 Kitchen dresser plan part 2.

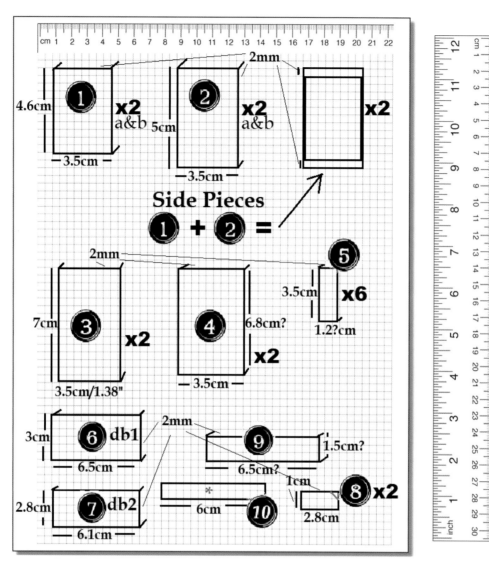

Fig 4 Plan for the optional wine rack/drawer section.

TOOLS AND MATERIALS

1. Workbench or secure worktop
2. Cutting mat, ideally placed on a solid surface, such as a workbench or secure and solid worktop
3. Thick bamboo skewers – 4mm in diameter
4. Thin bamboo skewers – 2–3mm in diameter

5. Pine wood panel sheet – approximately 250mm × 390mm × 4mm, which is enough to allow for errors
6. Five thinner pine wood panel sheets – approximately 250mm × 390mm × 2mm, enough to allow for errors
7. Square-cut wood rods – approximately 300mm × 12.6mm

8. Bamboo strips – approximately 400mm × 9mm × 3mm
9. Bamboo rods – approximately 5–6mm in diameter and 20cm long
10. Adhesives – wood glue (Crocodile) and Industrial-Grade superglue (Everbuild)
11. Decorlack acrylic paint in Glossy Black
12. Two-in-one sealant and varnish – Contura used here
13. Wood stain – Tableau Scratch Cover in Dark used here
14. Furniture repair pens
15. Liquitex Professional acrylic marker in Iridescent Antique Gold
16. Lip salve case (optional) – perfect for using as circle template for the cutout of the broken bonnet piece
17. Sharp pencil and metal ruler with finger guard
18. Weights (optional) – for weighting down flat pieces being glued together; alternatively, use heavy tins
19. Craft knife with spare blades – Stanley knife shown here

20. Small hammer and small craft nails – nails should be approximately 1cm long depending on the diameter of the beads used for finials and feet
21. Electric mini-mitre or cutoff saw (optional) – HaroldDol used here; this tool is inexpensive and can also be used for bulk cutting for miniature projects such as parquet flooring and wall panelling; alternatively, use a craft knife
22. Tapes – double-sided sticky tape, Tesa paper tape and 3M medical tape
23. Sanding sponges – coarse and fine
24. Curved file and needle files
25. Small handsaw or coping saw
26. Miniature hinges and drawer handles – 1:12 scale
27. Mixed wooden beads – 2–5mm in diameter for feet and finials
28. Sharp scissors (optional)
29. Scheppach electric scroll saw (optional; shown in Fig 6 overleaf) – for thicker pieces of wood; not used for this piece, which used thinner 2mm hand-cut pieces instead
30. Safety mask, goggles and gloves (not shown)

Fig 5 Workbench with all required tools and materials.

THE BROKEN BONNET TOP

A broken bonnet top, or broken arch top, on a piece of furniture is a vaguely bicorne hat-shaped (hence 'bonnet') top, with a break to the middle or to both sides of a middle section (hence 'broken bonnet'). The design was popular between the 1730s and 1780s, and was often used on cabinet furniture and highboys with turned and carved curved legs – Chippendale highboys, for example, often have a broken bonnet top incorporated into the design, together with cabriole legs. Original broken bonnet furniture and doorhead toppers can still be found in classical Georgian houses, much like those widely seen in Bath in the UK.

STEP-BY-STEP GUIDE

Cutting Out

Note: pieces marked on the plans with a question mark (nos 5 and 9 in Fig 6) should be cut as and when needed to the exact measurement, or else cut 5mm larger than stated initially then cut to exact size later.

1. Prepare to cut out the pieces, using Figs 4, 5 and (optionally) 6 as a guide. Place the wood panel sheets onto the cutting mat and work surface. Measure and draw out the pieces onto the wood panel. Label each piece of wood using with 3M or paper tape ready for cutting (Fig 7). Remember, all 4mm-thick pieces will need to be drawn and cut from both sides of the wood when cutting by hand with a craft knife. Thicker pieces of wood can also be cut with handsaw or coping saw, and crafters proficient in using an electric scroll saw may choose to use this.

   For cutting the no. 2 bamboo strips, the electric mini-mitre saw will prove invaluable, as it will reduce the time and energy required

Fig 6 A scroll saw.

Fig 7 Draw the pieces out on the wood, cut out and sand.

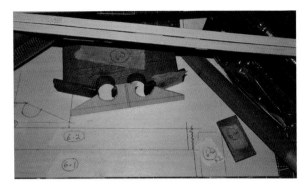

Fig 8 The top bonnet section.

Fig 9 A mini-mitre saw is a real time-saver for repetitive tasks.

(Fig 9); the same applies to cutting any bamboo sticks for decorating the door pieces.

When cutting curves, choose between a coping saw and a craft knife, depending on your skill level. For the purposes of this project, piece 6.3 was cut with a craft knife (Fig 8).

Sand any rough edges on all the cut pieces, using the curved and needle files to sand the broken bonnet circular spaces.

Outer Frame Assembly

2. For the back piece, use wood glue to fix the no. 2 bamboo strips to fill the no. 1 piece within the drawn border, as shown in Fig 10. Weight the piece down to ensure it dries flat. Once the glue has dried completely, sand the bamboo strips in order to remove any glue residue and create an even surface.

3. For the bottom and sides, use wood glue to fix the no.3 bottom piece and no. 4 side pieces flush with the outer border edges beside the now glued bamboo pieces, as shown in Fig 11. Use paper or 3M tape to hold the pieces in place while the glue dries. Use a sanding sponge or two (or a small box) to keep the pieces at right

Fig 10 Bamboo sticks on the back piece weighted down to dry.

Fig 11 Attaching the bottom and sides.

angles while drying. Do not worry if there is a slight gap between the fixed bottom and sides and the bamboo strips. Once the glue has completely dried, gently sand down the exterior joined areas so that the connections are smooth.

5. Fix the no. 5 middle worktop piece in place with wood glue, as shown in Fig 12.

6. Use superglue to fix top piece no. 6.2 to the middle of top piece 6.1 and hold together until set. Now fix the joined-together pieces to the top exposed edge of piece no. 1 with superglue (Fig 12), and hold in place until fixed. Apply a layer of wood glue to the internal edge and wipe smooth using a cotton bud or lint-free cloth.

7. Carefully position the no. 6.3 broken bonnet piece to the centre top (as far forward or back as desired) and fix in place with a layer of superglue. Add a layer of wood glue to the back of the broken bonnet piece and fix the no. 6.6 bamboo rod to the glued area so that it adds extra support to the upright broken bonnet piece once dried. If necessary, use 3M medical tape to hold the pieces in place while drying.

8. Now fix the no. 7 upper side pieces in place with wood glue, as shown in Fig 13. Use paper tape or

3M-type tape to hold them in place while drying if necessary. Once dry, gently sand to smooth any edges or gaps.

Shelves

9. To fit the interior shelves, start by gluing the no. 8.1 side spacers onto both sides, as shown in Fig 14. Once they are fixed, slot in the two no. 8 middle shelf pieces (they may need to be trimmed a little before sliding into place). The

Fig 12 Attaching the middle shelf, top, and broken bonnet.

Fig 13 Fitting the upper sides.

Fig 14 Fitting the shelves.

side spacers can be adjusted according to your shelf requirements – for example, you may wish to have just one central shelf to display larger pieces.

10. Once the shelves are fixed in place, add bamboo strip no. 9 to tidy the top interior space of the no. 1 back piece, and then the bottom no. 10 piece to tidy the bottom edge (both nos 9 and 10 pieces may need a slight trimming).

11. Glue the no. 9.4 bamboo rod pieces to the outer edge of each interior shelf with superglue (Fig 15). These will keep the display plates in position.

12. Fix the 9.1 edge pieces to each side of the shelf area with wood glue. When the glue is dry, overlay them with the 9.2 bamboo skewers cut to size to create a decorative carved effect (Fig 16). The outermost 9.2 pieces may need to be cut a little longer than the others to sit tidily against the worktop side.

Fig 15 Top and bottom interior trims and plate supports.

Fig 16 The front-facing edges.

Doors

The doors (no. 12) can be decorated as desired. The steps below are for the doors in this example.

13. Pieces 12.1 form the outer edges of each door. Use bamboo strips (no. 8 in the equipment list), cut in half lengthways or flat-edged meat skewers, as shown in Fig 17. Cut another identical strip of bamboo to size to place halfway between the now framed outer edges.

14. Cut the pointed tips of the bamboo skewers to fit between the horizontal strips with a craft knife or an electric mitre saw as in Fig 9, and then sand down and glue into place using either superglue gel (a small amount) or wood glue. Fig 17 also shows another more basic cross pattern as an alternative.

15. Colour the decorated doors with wood stain and/or scratch repair pens. For this piece the dark oak, mahogany and black pens were used. To give an older, more used look, apply a coat of black Decorlack gloss paint in between the pointed skewers. To give an even more aged appearance, as here, cut away tiny strips and rub down sections of the outer door frames with a craft knife and sanding sponge to create an uneven and worn look, then recolour these areas with wood stain.

16. Colour and stain the main body of the dresser using the same technique as for the doors and the earlier projects in this book. Figure 18 shows the colouring stage in progress; in this image, the optional bottle rack/drawer section is in place, as well as some additional beading to partner the bottle section.

17. Mark any areas you wish to stand out with the Liquitex gold marker. In this case, it was used on the front edges of the broken bonnet and lightly on the front of the middle shelves.

18. Once the colouring is complete, the doors can be fixed in place. The coloured no. 11 pieces will need to be fitted directly behind each of the doors so that they sit in the correct position when the doors are closed. Do not fix these until you have decided whether or not to make the optional middle section. If you do decide to include the wine rack section, add the no. 11 pieces as shown in Fig 19 (shown in bare wood for clarity) once the optional piece is complete, allowing approximately 1–2mm

Fig 17 Decorating the doors.

Fig 18 Colouring the main body of the dresser.

Fig 19 Fitting the door closure support pieces.

the handle into place; if necessary a tiny spot of superglue can be applied in the hole to strengthen the hold. A single hinge was then added to the central section of each door by applying superglue to the long hinge part and fixing it to the central wood strip in the middle of the door; then the small hinge part was fixed to the outer frame with small nails (making a small pilot hole into the outer frame first with a pointed needle file to prevent splitting), with the nails being hammered or pushed in to fix the hinge into place (Fig 20). Alternatively, the small hinge piece can simply be superglued to the side part of the cabinet so long as care is taken that no glue gets on the moving hinge section.

between the sides of the middle piece and the no. 11 pieces. The no. 11 pieces may need to be trimmed prior to fixing into place with a little wood glue.

19. Fix the desired hinges and door handles in place on each door half. For this example, a small William and Mary-style pull handle was added by making a small pilot hole (with a small pointed needle file) and then pushing

Hinges and handles for 1:12 scale miniatures can be found from specialist miniature makers and suppliers online. The hinges and handles used for this piece fitted the eighteenth-century theme and were chosen from a selection from Ulrike Wockauer of Ullis Puppenstube based in Bavaria and are available online (*see* appendices). Figure 21 shows a selection of 1:12 scale handles and hinges alongside a full-size William and Mary piece.

Fig 20 Example of a 1:12 scale hinge and handle fixture.

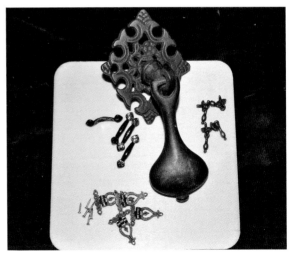

Fig 21 Selection of 1:12 scale hinges and drawer pulls.

Finishing Touches

20. For this piece, small wood beads were added to the broken bonnet section, with the smaller 1–2mm beads slotted onto small 25mm skewer spikes and glued in place.

21. To add feet, lay the cabinet flat on its back on the worktop and then make four pilot holes approximately 5mm in from each corner. Glue a 4mm bead onto each pilot hole with the bead hole showing up and centre. Once they are firmly glued, gently hammer or push (with the hammer) the correct length nail (about 7mm) into each bead to fully secure it into place.

22. A thin strip of half-cut ball beading was added to complement the optional bottle rack and drawer section. Another design could have been chosen, such as egg and dart, or trims and corbels can simply be bought from a miniature supplier.

23. Seal and varnish the dresser by applying a thin coat of two-in-one sealant/varnish to the whole piece, including doors, internal shelves, finials and behind-the-door sections with a small paintbrush. Leave to dry for the manufacturer's recommended drying time.

The dresser is now complete apart from the optional wine rack and drawer section, for which instructions are given below. Alternatively, the lower middle section could be left open to hold a basket or even store wood for the kitchen fire. One common use for such a space in a kitchen dresser in the eighteenth century would have been to store live fowl for laying eggs (often referred to as a 'coop dresser'); to recreate this, add some wooden upright bars with small spaces between them and then place a little straw behind them via one of the side doors.

Wine Rack and Drawer

24. Draw, cut out and sand the required pieces using Fig 6 as a guide, if not already done. The no. 5 and no. 9 pieces should only be cut when they are needed, to ensure accurate measurements.

25. Using wood glue, fix one of the side inner pieces no. 1a to the centre of side outer piece no. 2a so that there is a gap of approximately 2mm at each end (Fig 23). Repeat this process for two remaining 'b' pieces. Weight these down while drying to ensure the pieces are glued flat together.

26. Once the side pieces are completely dry, apply a layer of wood glue to the 2mm gaps at the top and bottom ends of both side pieces. Now fix the no. 3 top and bottom pieces in between the side pieces as shown in Fig 24. Wipe away any glue residue using a cotton bud or lint-free cloth. Use paper or 3M tape to secure the pieces together while the

Fig 22 The bottle rack and drawer combo.

Fig 23 The sides of the wine rack.

Fig 24 Fixing the wine rack bottom and top pieces.

Fig 25 Fixing the middle horizontals.

glue dries, and then place flat on the cutting mat with sanding sponges (or small boxes) to hold the shape of the piece while it dries completely.

27. The middle horizontal no. 4 pieces may need to be trimmed a little to fit (to approximately 6.8cm). There are various ways of fitting them:

Method 1: Lay the piece flat on the working mat and use some wood pieces that are approximately 12.5mm wide as positioning guides (the no. 11 wood pieces from Fig 5 are perfect for this), as shown in Fig 25. Fix the first shelf in place with superglue, then add another layer of no. 11-type positioning pieces and fix the second no. 4 horizontal in place. Once both no. 4 pieces are firmly fixed, slide out the positioning pieces.

Method 2: Measure three equal spaces from the interior bottom to the interior top and mark both sides to indicate where the no. 4 pieces will go.

Method 3: Another way to do this is to fix internal spacers as with the shelves for the main cabinet. More proficient miniature makers can simply cut grooves into the side pieces by hand or machine prior to fixing top and bottom pieces.

28. In order to slide the middle vertical no. 5 pieces snugly into place, either trim the previously oversized pieces or cut the pieces to the correct size now. In case of doubt, do a test run with a piece of cut card, effectively creating a template for each piece. Mark three dots at even intervals (divide the width by 4) on each side of the main frame as a guide to where to position each of the no. 5 pieces. Apply a small amount of wood glue to the outer long edges of each of piece and simply slide into place. Once the glue has dried, carefully file away any interior wood glue residue using a flat needle file.

29. To assemble the drawer, start by fixing the no. 7 drawer base 2 piece on top of drawer base 1 (no. 6) with wood glue so that it is centrally positioned between the short sides and flush with one of the long sides (which will be the front). This will leave a gap on the back long side and both short sides (Fig 26). Trim any uneven edges (especially on the front, flush side) and gently sand.

30. Once the base pieces are solidly fixed, stick the no. 8 side pieces in place using a little superglue applied to the gaps on each side of the drawer base (Fig 27 left). Glue the no. 10 bamboo piece to the back by applying glue to the gap

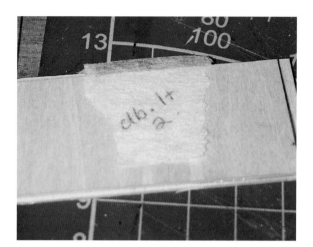

Fig 26 The drawer base before trimming and sanding.

on the back of the base and to the back of the no. 8 pieces.

32. Once the no. 8 and no. 10 pieces are fixed, use a craft knife to cut the side pieces down to join the bamboo back piece (Fig 27 right). Lay the sides flat onto the cutting mat and use a ruler as a guide to carefully cut at an angle. The angle doesn't need to be exact, as it's simply cosmetic and aids drawer insertion, but both sides should match. Gently sand any rough edges.

33. Before attaching the drawer front, carry out a dry run to see how much – if any – trimming is required by sliding the base into position in the main frame of the bottle/drawer piece and then placing the cut no. 9 piece into position without any adhesive. How much of the drawer should be cut away depends on whether you wish it to sit flush internally – as here – or against the outer frame. Trim the no. 9 piece to the desired size and then superglue it to the front of the drawer base and sides (Fig 28).

If you opt to cut the drawer front to the internal fit, it may be necessary to add a small strip of wood to the internal back space of the drawer section as shown in Fig 29. This will ensure that the drawer fits snuggly to the front of the piece and is held in place (slide the drawer into place to determine where to fix the strip of wood). Fig 29 shows the back of the piece prior to sanding and final adjustment and re-glueing of the horizontal and vertical pieces.

34. Sand the front of the drawer so that it has no rough edges. For more rounded, worn-looking corners, simply use a sanding sponge to soften the edges.

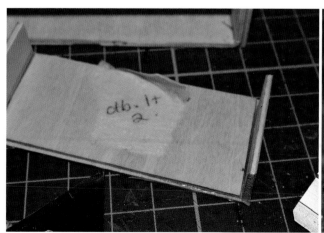

Fig 27 Joining the drawer sides and back.

Fig 28 Drawer front with an internal fit.

Fig 29 Drawer holder – prior to horizontal/vertical adjustments.

35. At this point, carry out final adjustments of the vertical and horizontal pieces and re-glue any pieces that have come loose. Once this final section is as desired (and remember it need not be perfect), give the whole piece a final sanding using the appropriate sanding sponge (fine) and needle files for inner spaces. Then stain it using the same techniques and materials chosen for the main cabinet so that it matches.

36. In this example, some handmade beading was added to the sides of the whole bottle rack/drawer section and then to the main cabinet to create a visual link between the two pieces (Fig 30). Of course, other decorative touches can be applied instead.

37. Place miniatures in the completed cabinet as desired, whether they be silver, pewter, ceramic or something else entirely. One simple way of ensuring that smaller pieces stay in place is to cut to size a small strip of wood (coloured to match the cabinet) and use some tacky tape to hold the miniatures onto the strip of wood; then simply place the wood strip and attached pieces onto the desired shelf area (Fig 31).

Fig 30 Attaching decorative beading.

Fig 31 Adding small accessories to the display.

CHAPTER 16

DISPLAY, PHOTOGRAPHY, CARE AND MAINTENANCE

This chapter provides some ideas on how to display and photograph your miniature pieces in creative and professional ways, as well as how to look after them.

BACKDROPS AND BASES

One way to display your miniatures is to use either printed backdrops or dioramas to establish a theme.

These types of wallpaper mural images are widely available online from sites such as eBay, Amazon, and interior furnishing and décor sites. Mural wallpaper is usually used for interior decorating at full scale (for our own homes), but on request sellers will usually provide a quote for resizing the whole mural to your required measurements. The two wallpaper murals shown were bought for around £30 each from Etsy sellers. The winter forest example was printed to a requested size of 130cm × 85cm and the black and white abbey print to a size of 120cm × 60cm. Often there is an option for the prints to come with an adhesive backing, which is useful, as it is best to attach the image to a large piece of plyboard so that it is kept flat and can be reused multiple times. You can even fix a different image to the other side of the plyboard to give you a choice and for efficient storage.

Scenic tapestries are also great to use as backdrops but can be a little more expensive; it's worth keeping an eye out for them at second-hand markets and car boot sales.

Outdoor backdrops such as gardens, brickwork, architecture, beaches and so on can provide the most beautiful settings. Always be aware of your surroundings and make sure to protect your miniatures when transporting to and from a natural setting. The zoomed-out image of the Fairy King project (*see* Chapter 12) shown here was taken in a garden. Fake grass or snow, or tiny pebbles and/or shells could also be used to enhance particular scenes.

DIGITAL BACKDROPS

You can also add a background digitally, after photographing the miniature (ideally in a plain white setting). Use an app or online software solution such as removebg to completely remove any background around your miniatures and then replace it with your own background or again use software (such as designify) to create a forest, clouds, pastels or whatever is desired. Both removebg and designify offer free use for certain downloads (correct at time of print), but you may find newer or better versions of these by searching online for 'free photograph background removal', for example.

Wallpaper mural for an abbey theme.

Snowy forest wallpaper mural.

Tapestry wall hanging.

An outdoor setting.

Examples for the display floor.

Create your own base boards to sit your miniatures upon for photographing. These could be made is the same way as the wallpaper mural boards, but you can also add printed tile sheets or even real miniature tiles, stone flooring or wooden floorboards. Tiles, floorboards, stone flags and so on can all be found in 1:12 scale on Etsy or from miniature artisans and are often available in both real (actual stone/ceramic/wood/marble) or printed formats.

CABINETS, DISPLAY CASES AND STANDS

Fantasy, themed pieces and standalone items can look wonderful when displayed under a glass dome or cloche. You can also find glass display boxes (often up to the size of a small fish tank) either old or new; these were very popular during the Victorian era.

A wooden stand is often great for photographing and/or displaying a piece that you wish to raise up to give a better perspective. The wooden stand and plinth shown here is a salvage piece from the 1900s which would have originally had its own bell jar to sit atop it. Finds like this make beautiful display pieces.

Miniatures are made to be admired, but there are times when you will need to keep them in storage; perhaps you are making items to sell, or you simply have a collection that you dip into and change around now and again. One way to both admire and store multiple miniatures is to invest in a larger display cabinet that can hold many pieces but still offers a display visual. Examples are shown here. Such items are readily available from home furnishing catalogues or online, and are easy to embellish with a top piece or tassel for an antique feel.

A simple doored cabinet without glass will suffice if you simply need to store items (rather than display

Display and storage ideas.

them) and protect them from dust or contaminants such as paints and adhesives.

Other simple ways of displaying your miniatures include using glass lanterns or candle holders, which again can be found online or at antique markets.

If you need to put items into storage but don't have any of the cabinets or display options mentioned, simply wrap up the pieces carefully in lint-free fabric or some tissue paper and store them away in a strong lidded container until later.

COLLECTOR'S CABINET

The Rijksmuseum in Amsterdam is home to this beautiful display cabinet from 1730, filled with many miniature pots, bottles, fossils, wood samples and more besides (much like a dolls' house). Such pieces are in themselves beautiful works of art and an inspiration for making your own display cases.

Collector's cabinet with miniature apothecary, 1730. (Rijksmuseum, Amsterdam)

PHOTOGRAPHY

You do not have to be an expert in photography in order to capture some beautiful images of your miniatures, as modern cameras and even smartphones have the ability to capture very good quality images with very little expertise required. This is great because it enables us to focus on being visual learners and experimenters. Mobile phones are perfect for capturing images that you happen on by chance (and therefore don't have your camera with you). The camera used for most of the images shown in this book is an Olympus OMD E-M10 II which is now a few years old. If buying your own camera, try to find one that has a good zoom capability and allows for manual use, which will give you control over your image shots when it comes to variables such as lighting, zoom and positional dynamics.

Investing is some basic photographic studio lighting kit is worthwhile if you intend to regularly photograph your work for both personal and commercial applications. It's not essential to have, but eliminates issues with daylight (especially in the winter), sorts out shadows and, most importantly, helps to highlight wood detail such as patterns and carvings on darker pieces. Starter kits are available from around £60 on Amazon and usually include two extendable tripods with umbrella reflective lamps (with energy-saving bulbs) and a carrier. You can also find full studio kits with green screens and backdrops, but these extra features will be reflected in the price.

Create a workspace for taking your photographs, for example a small table area or the top of an unused fireplace, ideally fitted flush against a wall so that you can sit any background imagery against it (such as the mural wallpaper mentioned above). Place your chosen floor covering (tiles, snow, grass or a plain piece of fabric, for example) on the flat top of your workspace.

When photographing miniatures, you may wish to take some pictures that include full-size objects beside them to give an indication of scale – for example boots, a bottle of wine, a cup and saucer or an apple – or use an actual measuring tool such as a ruler. A wonderful way to personalise miniature photography is to include your own pets, which gives a wonderful scale comparison at the same

Basic photographic lighting kit.

time; just be mindful of small parts. Last but not least, you can simply photograph the piece in your own hand or have your face or arm looking towards the miniature or miniature scene.

CLEANING

Never hoover anywhere near a miniature, as many a piece will simply disappear into that black hole and some pieces will never be found again, no matter how many times you sift through your hoover bag. You can blow dust away yourself or purchase a can of duster air; the best types for this are the ones that are used for cleaning computer keyboards, as these are not too powerful and often have a straw applicator that you can use to get into small areas to blow away any accumulated dirt. These are also perfect for areas you do not want to risk using fluids

on, such as paper coverings, delicate fabrics and/or any fragile additions.

Use a tiny amount of non-chemical soap and water (damp lint-free) and wipe dry with lint-free cloths. Leave to air dry completely and then wrap items in cotton, silk or linen offcuts; use offcuts that you do not mind getting wood stain on, as there can sometimes be a natural transfer between the touching pieces.

A mixture of half a glass of Heinz cleaning vinegar and half a glass of olive oil works wonders in cleaning wood (use circular motions, again with a lint-free cloth). For smaller pieces, use a cotton bud.

STORAGE

Store miniatures that are not in use or on display in sealed boxes in a dry and clean area that is out of direct light. Add a silica moisture absorber bag to the box – these are often found in delivered goods and can simply be reused. Dropping an incense cone into the storage box (for example frankincense and myrrh) will give your miniatures a slight scent; alternatively, add a piece of card scented with your favourite perfume or some wooden mothballs, which often have a lavender scent, and will also help to keep away unwanted visitors.

You can often recycle packaging to store your miniatures. Tic Tac boxes, for example, are great for small parts. Large packs of dishwasher or laundry tablets often come in upright biodegradable containers that are perfect for paintbrushes and for wood edging pieces (usually these containers have a paper outer that is removable and recyclable with your paper waste). Any old or antique boxes you have at home can also be repurposed to store miniatures, which saves buying new.

When buying boxes, try to choose recyclable ones. There are many brands available, but the ones I use are called Really Useful Storage boxes, which are great for stacking and storing miniatures and miniature-making materials. These boxes are 100 per cent recyclable and are a cost-effective way to store items safely and tidily.

The completed projects in this book.

SUPPLIERS OF EQUIPMENT AND MATERIALS

Patrizia Bellini
Berlin, Germany
Etsy shop: Landolina
www.etsy.com/shop/Landolina
Coaster tiles

Bromley Craft Products Ltd
PO Box 283
Uckfield
East Sussex TN22 9DY
Telephone: 01825 732515
www.craft-products.com/mouldings.php
Online suppliers of dolls' house
mouldings and timber

DandyLion Miniatures
www.dandylionminiatures.com

Dolls House Cottage Workshop
Sawley Marina
Sawley
Long Eaton
Nottingham NG10 3AE
Telephone: 0115 946 5059
www.dollshousemouldings.com
Online shop for architecturally correct Victorian
and Georgian mouldings (cornices, covings,
skirting etc). To visit the showroom, call ahead
for an appointment

Farrow & Ball
Uddens Estate
Wimborne
Dorset BH21 7NL
Telephone: 01202 876141
www.farrow-ball.com
Perfect period paint colours in tester pot sizes, as
well as period colour papers for walls

Melody Jane Dolls' Houses Ltd
Cambrian
Bryn Road
Towyn
Abergele
Conwy LL22 9HN
Telephone: 01745 330072
www.melodyjane.com/
dolls-house-builders-merchants
Mouldings, trims, timber and hardware such as
door handles

The Miniature Scene of York
Telephone: 01904 638265
https://miniaturescene.com
Great for mouldings, corbels and so on, as well as
beautiful wooden Tudor candle lighting and
candles that are pre-wired and perfect to add to
your miniatures

Lisa Morrow
California, USA
Etsy shop: MidDreamers
www.etsy.com/shop/MidDreamers
Fairy artisan

Tiny Ceramics
Im Silbertal 5
56203 Höhr-Grenzhausen
Germany
www.tiny-ceramics.com
Tiny tiles available in many colours as well as
     mural tile kits

Ullis Puppenstube
Falkensteinstrasse 1
94577 Winzer
Bavaria
www.ullis-puppenstube.de
www.etsy.com/shop/ulliskreativeecke
1:12 scale miniatures, needlework, accessories
     and supplies, including miniature drawer and
     door handles

Viorica
Netherlands
Etsy shop: Miniatures By Vio
www.miniaturesbyvio.etsy.com
Working window kits

Zjakazumi
Sokolniki, Poland
www.etsy.com/shop/ZjakazumiDolls
Ball-jointed dolls in 1:12 and 1:24 scales

PLACES OF INTEREST TO VISIT

Bowood House and Gardens
Derry Hill
Calne
Wiltshire SN11 0LZ
Telephone: 01249 812102
www.bowood.org

Castell Coch
Cardiff CF15 7JS
Telephone: 03000 252239
https://cadw.gov.wales/visit/places-to-visit/
    castell-coch#contact-us

Chavenage House
Tetbury
Gloucestershire GL8 8XP
Telephone: 01666 502329
https://chavenage.com

Hever Castle and Gardens
Hever Road
Edenbridge
Kent TN8 7NG
Telephone: 01732 865224
www.hevercastle.co.uk

Ilkley Toy Museum
2 Whitton Croft Road
Ilkley
West Yorkshire LS29 9HR
Telephone: 01943 603855/07808 762982
www.ilkleytoymuseum.co.uk/collection/

Jane Austen's House Museum
Winchester Road
Chawton
Alton
Hampshire GU34 1SD
Telephone: 01420 83262
www.jane-austens-house-museum.org.uk

Kensington Dollshouse Festival
Kensington Town Hall
Hornton Street
London W8 7NX
Telephone: 020 7812 9892
https://dollshouseshowcase.com

Madurodam
George Maduroplein 1
2584 RZ The Hague
The Netherlands
Telephone: +31 70 41 624 00
www.madurodam.nl/en
The city in miniature (and so much more)

Metropolitan Museum of Art
1000 5th Avenue
New York
USA
www.metmuseum.org

The Miniatura Show
Telephone: 0121 783 9922
https://miniatura.co.uk

Mouseman Visitor Centre
Kilburn
York YO61 4AH
Telephone: 01347 869100
www.robertthompsons.co.uk/visitor-centre/

Newstead Abbey
Ravenshead
Nottinghamshire NG15 8NA
Satnav: NG15 9HJ
Telephone: 0115 876 3100
https://newsteadabbey.org.uk
Monastic abbey from the late twelfth century and
    former home of Romantic poet Lord Byron

No. 1 Royal Crescent
1 Royal Crescent
Bath BA1 2LR
Telephone: 01225 428126
https://no1royalcrescent.org.uk

Palazzo Medici Riccardi
Via Camillo Cavour
Florence
Italy
www.palazzo-medici.it

Pollock's Toy Museum
1 Scala Street
London W1T 2HL
Telephone: 020 7636 3452
www.pollockstoymuseum.co.uk

Rjiksmuseum
Museumstraat 1
1071 XX Amsterdam
The Netherlands
Telephone: +31 20 674 7000
www.rijksmuseum.nl/nl

St Fagans National Museum of History
Cardiff CF5 6XB
Telephone: 029 2057 3500
https://museum.wales/stfagans/

Tithe Barn
Cumhill Farm
Pilton
Somerset BA4 4BG
https://en.wikipedia.org/wiki/Tithe_Barn,_Pilton
Often used for medieval fairs

Tower of London
North Bank
London EC3N 4AB
Telephone: +44 333 320 6000
www.hrp.org.uk/tower-of-london

Toy Worlds Museum Basel
Steinenvorstadt 1
CH-4051 Basel
Switzerland
Telephone: +41 61 225 95 95
www.spielzeug-welten-museum-basel.ch/de/

Tudor Merchant's House
Quay Hill
Tenby
Pembrokeshire SA70 7BX
Telephone: 01646 623110
www.nationaltrust.org.uk/tudor-merchants-house

Vatican Museums
Viale Vaticano
00120 Vatican City
Italy
www.museivaticani.va

Victoria & Albert Museum
Cromwell Road
London SW7 2RL
Telephone: 020 7942 2000
www.vam.ac.uk

Windsor Castle
Windsor
Berkshire SL4 1NJ
Telephone: 020 7766 7304
windsorcastle.co.uk

Young V&A
Cambridge Heath Road
Bethnal Green
London E2 9PA
Telephone: 020 8983 5200
www.vam.ac.uk/young

FURTHER READING

Bird, Lonnie, *Taunton's Complete Illustrated Guide to Period Furniture Details* (Taunton Press Inc., 2003)

Conover, Ernie, *The Lathe Book: A Complete Guide to the Machine and its Accessories* (Taunton Press Inc., 2020)

Denyer-Baker, Pauline, *Painting Miniatures* (The Crowood Press, 2014)

Dollhouse Miniatures magazine, www.dhminiatures.com

Dollshouse World magazine, https://dollshouseworld.com

Dunn, Tim, *Model Villages* (Amberley Publishing, 2017)

Emery, Anthony, *Greater Medieval Houses of England and Wales, 1300–1500: Volume 1, Northern England* (Cambridge University Press, 1996)

Emery, Anthony, *Greater Medieval Houses of England and Wales, 1300–1500: Volume 2, East Anglia, Central England and Wales* (Cambridge University Press, 2000)

Fleming, Stephen, *The Leather Crafting, Wood Burning and Whittling Starter Handbook* (2020)

Hiller, Nancy R., *English Arts & Crafts Furniture: Projects & Techniques for the Modern Maker* (Popular Woodworking Books, 2018)

Laier, Tony and Kate, *Get Started in Leather Crafting* (Design Originals, 2017)

Skeels, Rebecca, *Soldering for Jewellers* (The Crowood Press, 2017)

Stanley, Jeff, *Pyrography: A Beginner's Guide to Learning Wood Burning Techniques and Patterns* (2021)

Stapleford, Richard, *Lorenzo de' Medici at Home: The Inventory of the Palazzo Medici in 1492* (Pennsylvania State University Press, 2013)

Stickley, Gustav, *Making Authentic Craftsman Furniture: Instructions and Plans for 62 Projects* (Dover Woodworking, 1986)

Wenham, Martin, *The Art of Letter Carving in Wood* (The Crowood Press, 2022)

INDEX

First published in 2023 by
The Crowood Press Ltd
Ramsbury, Marlborough
Wiltshire SN8 2HR

enquiries@crowood.com

www.crowood.com

British Library Cataloguing-in-Publication Data
A catalogue record for this book is available from the
British Library.

ISBN 978 0 7198 4275 7

Dedication
I dedicate this book to all the time travellers and dreamers,
the believers in the impossible, the forever young with
old souls and to the miniaturists, carpenters, and artisans
and to all the mothers and fathers that bring art into their
children's lives (including mine, Irene and Barry); to Denise
for being my forever grown-up sister; to Lulu, Tig and
Flatty for the adventures; and, most importantly, to my
Steve for his courage, his advice and his still water.

Acknowledgements
A special thank you I give to Helen Francis of Hever Castle
for making my first approach to one of the UK's great
treasures such a simple process. I also give a huge thanks
to all the miniaturists and artisans who share their art
and encourage others to continue in their craft allowing
human creativity/expression/interaction/individuality to
thrive, be seen and be heard.

Typeset by Simon and Sons
Cover design by Sergey Tsvetkov
Printed and bound in India by Parksons Graphics Pvt. Ltd.